POPULATION GROWTH

Judith E. Jacobsen
Environmental Policy
and Management Program
University of Denver

UNIVERSITY SCIENCE BOOKS
SAUSALITO, CALIFORNIA

University Science Books
55D Gate Five Road
Sausalito, CA 94965
Fax: (415) 332-5393

Managing Editor: Lucy Warner
Editor: Louise Carroll
NCAR Graphics Team: Justin Kitsutaka, Lee Fortier, Wil Garcia,
Barbara Mericle, David McNutt, and Michael Shibao
Cover Design and Photography: Irene Imfeld
Compositor: Archetype Typography, Berkeley, California

This book is printed on acid-free paper.

Library of Congress Catalog Number: 95-061064

ISBN: 0-935702-81-4

Printed in the United States of America

10 9 8 7 6 5 4 3 2 1

POPULATION
GROWTH

A Note on the Global Change Instruction Program

This series has been designed by college professors to fill an urgent need for interdisciplinary materials on the emerging science of global change. These materials are aimed at undergraduate students not majoring in science. The modular materials can be integrated into a number of existing courses —in earth sciences, biology, physics, astronomy, chemistry, meteorology, and the social sciences. They are written to capture the interest of the student who has little grounding in math and the technical aspects of science but whose intellectual curiosity is piqued by concern for the environment. The material presented here should occupy about two weeks of classroom time.

For a complete list of modules available in the Global Change Instruction Program, contact University Science Books, Sausalito, California, fax (415) 332-5393. Information about the Global Change Instruction Program is also available on the World Wide Web at http://home.ucar.edu/ucargen/education/gcmod/contents.html.

Contents

Preface

This module on population growth is the first Global Change Instruction Program contribution that deals substantively with a body of knowledge outside the physical sciences. Its presence acknowledges the complex nature of global change—that it is composed of intertwining physical, biological, and chemical processes on the one hand and human activity in all its social and political complexity on the other. Its presence is also testament to the powerful role that population growth plays in global change.

Dealing as it does with demography, parts of this module involve quantities—numbers of people, numbers of births, rates of growth. But more often this module involves qualities—ideas, equities, advantages, and disadvantages. Teachers and students more accustomed to handling quantities are urged to relax none of their critical faculties: the commerce in qualitative ideas can be valid or invalid, convincing or not, logical or not. But they are urged to ease up on the notion that the only valid ideas are precise ones.

Judith E. Jacobsen
University of Denver

Acknowledgments

This instructional module has been produced by the the Global Change Instruction Program of the Advanced Study Program of the National Center for Atmospheric Research, with support from the National Science Foundation. Any opinions, findings, conclusions, or recommendations expressed in this publication are those of the author and do not necessarily reflect the views of the National Science Foundation.

Executive Editors: John W. Firor, John W. Winchester

Global Change Working Group

Louise Carroll, University Corporation for Atmospheric Research

Arthur A. Few, Rice University

John W. Firor, National Center for Atmospheric Research

David W. Fulker, University Corporation for Atmospheric Research

Judith Jacobsen, University of Denver

Lee Kump, Pennsylvania State University

Edward Laws, University of Hawaii

Nancy H. Marcus, Florida State University

Barbara McDonald, National Center for Atmospheric Research

Sharon E. Nicholson, Florida State University

J. Kenneth Osmond, Florida State University

Jozef Pacyna, Norwegian Institute for Air Research

William C. Parker, Florida State University

Glenn E. Shaw, University of Alaska

John L. Streete, Rhodes College

Stanley C. Tyler, University of California, Irvine

Lucy Warner, University Corporation for Atmospheric Research

John W. Winchester, Florida State University

This project was supported, in part, by the
National Science Foundation
Opinions expressed are those of the authors and not necessarily those of the Foundation

POPULATION
GROWTH

INTRODUCTION
Population and Global Change

For many centuries, scientists have observed with concern the changes in the natural world brought about by human activities. Ancient Greeks noticed that cutting forests muddied and dried up water courses. Victorian Britons watched plants and animals die within close range of smokestacks. Rachel Carson drew our attention to the harm done to certain bird species by synthetic pesticides.

In the last few decades, the human-induced changes have reached a severity, rapid pace, and geographic scale that is mobilizing unprecedented concern and action. Indeed, the constellation of changes in the natural world wrought by the human hand are seen now to amount to a global-scale force and are called collectively "global change" or "global environmental change."

Global change has many aspects. Most commonly included in it are deforestation, loss of species, degradation of soils and vegetation, contamination of both fresh water and the oceans, a rise in sea level, and air pollution (including an increase in certain heat-trapping gases in the atmosphere that may raise average atmospheric temperature). It is widely felt that human societies will have to respond to these changes in some way—by adapting to them, ameliorating them, and preventing further change—in order to avoid serious harm.

One well-documented phenomenon that has accompanied global change and interacts with each of its aspects in complex ways is the topic of this module: the rapid rise in the size of the human population on Earth. It took all of human history prior to 1800—all of the four or five million years since human-like creatures first appeared—for the number of people on Earth to reach one billion. The second billion appeared in 130 years. It took 30 years for the third billion, 15 years for the fourth billion, and just 12 years for the fifth billion to establish itself on Earth. Figure 1 presents this population history graphically. In 1992 we numbered more than 5.4 billion—92 million more people than in 1991, another Mexico and Denmark combined—and we continue to grow.

The Earth's human population interacts with the physical world in numerous ways to produce the impacts on the local, regional, and global environment that can add up to global change. It is possible to simplify consideration of these interactions by dividing the impact into two parts: the number of people and the activity per person that is related to global change. In the case of industrial pollution, the formula is: total impact = (number of people) x (pollution per person). In the case of nonindustrial activity such as land degradation from overgrazing, the formula is: total impact = (number of people) x (activity per person).

The formulas tell us that if we wish to curb global change, we will have to curb growth in the numbers of people and in pollution per person, and we will have to change nonindustrial activities that contribute to global change to make them less harmful. The following exercise illustrates some of the interactions among these elements.

Exercise

The world's 1992 population of 5.4 billion people placed approximately 6 billion tons of carbon, in the form of carbon dioxide, into the atmosphere annually. It is expected that this alteration of atmospheric composition will lead to a warming of the global climate. Annual output of carbon dioxide per person *on average* is 1.11 billion tons. (Remember, averaging lumps the United States with countries like Nepal and Mali, countries with vastly different contributions of carbon dioxide to the atmosphere.)

1. What would be the total amount of carbon dioxide added to the atmosphere annually at current per capita production levels if

   a. world population stabilizes at 10 billion, an optimistic view;

   b. world population stabilizes at 11.6 billion, which current United Nations projections include as a reasonable possibility; and

   c. world population stabilizes at 14 billion, which some analysts fear is most likely of all.

2. By how much would per capita consumption of carbon dioxide have to be reduced to keep total production at 6 billion tons annually under each of the three population scenarios above?

3. What would per capita production of carbon dioxide have to be under each population scenario in order to halve annual global emissions?

Describe the results of your calculations verbally and present your numbers in tabular form.

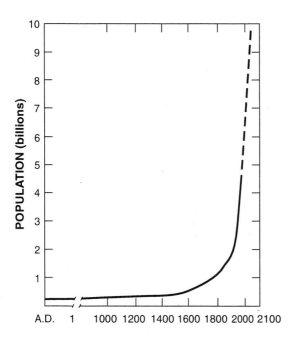

Figure 1. World population in history. From World Development Report 1984, *by the World Bank, Oxford University Press, 1984. Reprinted by permission.*

Discussion

Current emissions of carbon dioxide to the atmosphere are overpowering the planet's natural mechanisms for absorbing and assimilating the gas—the steadily increasing atmospheric concentration is evidence of this. Thus the question is, what will it take to decrease annual emissions? This exercise illustrates the role of population growth in answering that question.

In Question 1, one assumes steady per capita emissions and finds, of course, that emissions increase with continued population growth—the more people, the more emissions. Even this scenario would require change in current trends: *per capita* emissions have been growing, not stabilizing, and the understandable ambitions of populous Third World countries to improve the circumstances of their citizens will accelerate that trend.

In Question 2, we ask what would be required to stabilize *emissions* at current levels (where, remember, atmospheric concentrations would still continue to increase). Even with the optimistic estimate of 10 billion people, per capita emissions would have to be cut nearly in half. Higher populations, of course, require even more dramatic cuts in per capita emissions to achieve stable total emissions. Such cuts would require very rapid increases in the efficiency with which we use fossil fuels and forests or, in the alternative, major economic depressions and widespread increases in poverty.

Finally, in Question 3, we approach the actions needed to stabilize the *composition* of the atmosphere (approximated by a 50% cut in total emissions). Here, per capita emissions must go to 27% of their present value if population grows to 10 billion, to 25% at a population of 11.6 billion, and to 19% at the highest population of 14 billion. Such changes would require the industrial world to adopt all techniques available for improving efficiency; make major changes in the direction of simpler,

less-consuming ways of life; and replace fossil fuels with other energy sources rapidly. In the developing world, all the efficiency, appropriate technology, and alternative fuels possible would be required for standards of living to improve at all while halving total emissions. Once again, the difficulties are amplified by population growth.

* * *

In this module, we will seek understanding of how human populations behave. We will consider which countries have populations that are growing rapidly in the world today, which countries are growing slowly, and why; the driving forces of population growth and high fertility; and the prospects for slowing growth and eventually stabilizing world population. This material will give us a better understanding of the interaction between population growth and human activities that produces global change and will allow better-informed evaluation of prospects for curbing global change.

I
Demographic Basics

Of the many important elements in the study of population, or demography, five are critical to an understanding of population growth and global change. They are: (1) growth rates, or how the population of a country or the world is growing or, in some cases, decreasing; (2) birth rates, or fertility, the plus side of the equation—the rate at which people are being added to the population; (3) zero population growth, or population stabilization, known in technical demography as population stationarity; (4) death rates, or mortality, the minus side of the population equation; and (5) age-sex structure of the population. Each of these is discussed in this section.

In the discussion that follows, examples will be given from around the world as of mid-1992. The source for nearly all figures is the 1992 World Population Data Sheet published by the Population Reference Bureau in Washington, D.C. The most recent data sheet accompanies this module as an Appendix.

A country's population grows to the extent that births plus in-migrants exceed deaths plus out-migrants. The growth rate is usually given as a percentage—the number of people added to a population in a year divided by the size of that population, usually at midyear.

When migration is ignored, the growth rate is called **natural increase**. Migration is frequently ignored in discussions of population growth, and the growth rates most commonly discussed are rates of natural increase. It is always necessary, when discussing the natural increase of a particular country, to remember that the migration component is missing. Net migration into some countries is a significant piece of total growth. In the United States, for example, where the rate of natural increase in 1992 was 0.8% a year, total immigration, both legal and illegal, was estimated conservatively to increase the total growth rate by approximately a third, to over 1.0% annually. Of course, migration between countries is irrelevant to the global population growth rate.

The world as a whole was experiencing an annual natural increase of 1.7% in 1992. Within that aggregate number, rates varied from a high of 4.6% in Gaza to a low of –0.2% in Hungary. In general, the highest growth rates in the world, as in every year for some time, were in Africa. These include 3.8% in Zambia, 3.7% in Kenya, and 3.6% in Cote d'Ivoire. The Third World as a whole grew by 2.0%. Excluding China, which has a relatively low growth rate for its level of wealth, the annual natural increase rate for the developing world in 1992 was 2.3%. (The terms "Third World" and "developing world" are used interchangeably in this module.)

Developed countries grew on average at 0.5%. Nearly all European countries, Russia, Ukraine, Belarus, and Japan had increase rates of less than 0.5% a year, while the rest of the developed world, including the United States, Canada, Australia, and New Zealand, exceeded that rate. Two countries, Germany and Hungary, had negative growth rates in 1992; one, Bulgaria, had exactly zero growth.

Another way to consider growth rate is to translate it into a **doubling time**, the years required for a population to double in size if its annual growth rate were to continue unchanged. (Another module in this series, *System*

Behavior and System Modeling, by Arthur Few, discusses growth rates and doubling times.) A complicated formula is required to make this calculation precisely, but an approximation is to divide the annual growth rate into 70. Thus the world as a whole would double in just over 41 years if it continued to grow at the 1992 rate of 1.7% annually. In 1992 the developing world including China was growing fast enough to double in 34 years; Zambia's growth rate means a very short doubling time of a little more than 18 years.

Birth rates are expressed in a number of ways, but the most meaningful to many people is what is called the **total fertility rate**, or TFR. The TFR is a statistical creation that generalizes from the fertility behavior of a population of women in a particular year to their entire lifetimes. The result is an average number of children per woman. TFR in the United States, for example, had risen to 2.0 by 1992, meaning that if women were to behave throughout their childbearing lifetimes as they behaved in 1992, they would on average have two children. In the developed world as a whole, TFR was 1.9 in 1992. Figures for individual developed countries ranged from 1.2 in Hong Kong, 1.3 in Italy and Spain, and 1.4 in Germany and Portugal to 2.0 in the United States and Poland, 2.2 in Ireland, and 2.3 in Iceland.

In the developing world, TFRs in 1992 went as high as 8.0, in Rwanda, but averaged 3.8 children per woman (when China is included) and 4.4 (excluding China). Women in Asia and Latin America averaged between three and four children, while women in Africa had just over six.

A useful notion when talking about fertility rates is **replacement fertility**, the number of children that parents need to have for a generation to replace itself. This number is roughly two children, one for each parent, but the precise number depends on the pattern of deaths in a population: because some people die before reproducing themselves, TFRs slightly above 2.0 are required to compensate for these deaths.

Replacement fertility is actually 2.1 children per woman in the United States, while it is in the neighborhood of 2.3 in India.

Discounting immigration for the moment to highlight a point about fertility, a country with fertility at or below replacement will eventually stabilize its population when births equal deaths, or zero population growth is achieved. *Eventually* is the critical word; the actual dynamics of below-replacement fertility and zero population growth will be discussed below.

Another commonly used birth rate is the **crude birth rate** (CBR), the number of births per 1,000 people in a population. Crude birth rates in 1992 ranged from 52 and 53 in several African countries to 10, 11, and 12 in some European countries. The CBR in the United States was 16 in 1992. Though CBR does not have the familiarity and obvious meaning that the notion of "four children per woman" has, it is used widely.

Death rates, or mortality, can be expressed in a number of ways. The **crude death rate** (CDR) corresponds to the crude birth rate. It is the number of deaths per 1,000 people in a population. CDRs ranged in 1992 from 23 in Guinea-Bissau, in West Africa, to 5 in Japan and several other countries. (See the system modeling module for an explanation of the use of CBR and CDR to calculate rate of natural increase.)

Other death rates include age-specific death rates, or rate of death at particular ages. One especially useful age-specific death rate is the **infant mortality rate**, or the number of infants per 1,000 born alive that die before their first birthdays. This is an extremely sensitive indicator of well-being in a society and tells us more than crude death rates alone. The lowest infant mortality rate in the world in 1992 was in Japan, where 4.6 infants died in the first year of life out of every 1,000 born. In contrast, in the United States, high infant mortality among the poor kept the rate at 9.0, which is high for a wealthy country but low compared to the developing world, which as a whole had an infant mortality rate more than nine times that. Furthermore, in the poorer parts of Africa, the rate *averages* something over 100 and can reach as high as 200–250 in some regions of some countries. An infant mortality rate of 250 means that one out of every four babies born alive dies before reaching age one.

Another useful age-specific death rate is the **child death rate**, defined as the annual number of deaths before the fifth birthday per 1,000 live births. Child death rates in 1988 ranged from 300 in Afghanistan to 7 in Finland. In the United States, 13 children per 1,000 born alive died before reaching age five. Thirty countries are considered by the United Nations Children's Fund (UNICEF) to have "very high" child mortality rates, above 170; another 30 have "high" rates of between 95 and 170. Child death rates include infant mortality, but they

also capture deaths among children in the vulnerable years just after they are weaned, when an increase in deaths can occur.

A final death rate of importance to a discussion of population issues around the world is the **maternal mortality rate**. Defined as the annual number of deaths of women from pregnancy-related causes per 100,000 live births, in 1988 it ranged from 1,700 in Bhutan to 2 in Norway, according to UNICEF. Many countries do not report or gather maternal mortality data; among those that do, three in addition to Bhutan had rates of 1,000 or above in 1988: Somalia, Ghana, and the Congo. Eighteen countries, mostly in Europe, North America, East Asia, and Oceania, had single-digit maternal mortality rates.

The last important element of demography

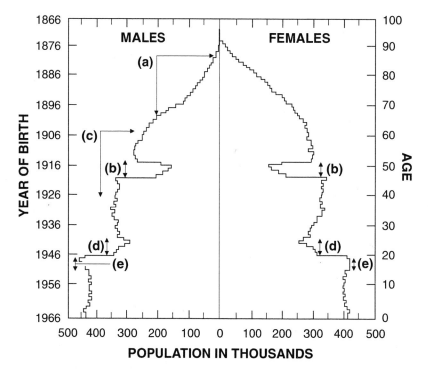

Figure 2. Population of France, by age and sex, in 1968. (a) and (c) indicate military losses in World Wars I and II, respectively; (b) and (d) are the slowing of birth rates during those wars; (e) is the "baby boom" after World War II. From The Methods and Materials of Demography, *by Henry S. Shryock and Jacob S. Siegel, Academic Press, 1973. Reprinted by permission.*

to be discussed here is **age-sex structure**. The age and sex composition of a population is easily presented in what is called a **population pyramid**. Such a diagram shows how many people of each sex there are of every age—or, usually, every five-year age group. The horizontal axis is usually the number of people or the percentage of the population; the vertical axis is usually age or year of birth. (See the system modeling module for an exercise in constructing an age-sex pyramid.)

The population pyramid for France as of 1968, shown in Figure 2, illustrates that it is possible, from such a diagram, to trace the demographic history of a country. The letters below correspond to letters on the diagram, from which we can see the following:

a. More women than men had lived to old age. This is because of male deaths in World War I (men born in the 1880s and 1890s would be in their 20s and 30s during World War I), in addition to the usual female longevity observed in most of the world.

b. Fertility fell during World War I.

c. Male deaths during World War II again reduced the number of men compared with women.

d. Fertility fell again during World War II.

e. Fertility then boomed after World War II—even more dramatically than after World War I.

A population's structure reveals something of its future. Figure 3 shows stylized population pyramids for a high-fertility country, A, that has not yet experienced a fertility decline, a country, B, that has gone from relatively high fertility to below replacement quickly, and a third country, C, whose fertility has been low for a long time. In country A, there are many

more children than older people. When those children grow up to become parents (imagine the pyramid scrolling up its vertical axis like the picture on a computer screen), they will contribute a lot of population growth even if they each have fewer children than their parents did. The size of the base of the pyramid shows that the potential for future population growth is enormous in country A. Several African countries have similar population pyramids.

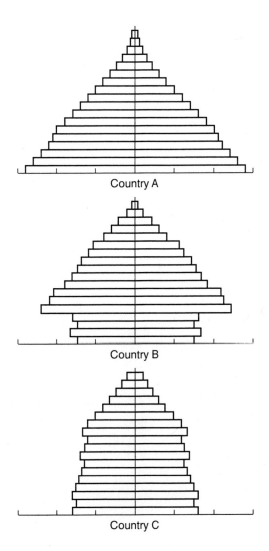

Figure 3. Stylized age-sex pyramids for three hypothetical countries.

Fertility has fallen in country B, but quite recently and after a "baby boom." Country B will not have zero population growth until this bulge of people ages, scrolling up the pyramid, and the number of births equals the number of deaths.

Thus it is because of age structure that replacement fertility does not necessarily yield zero population growth. The United States, for example, will not experience zero population growth until the baby-boom generation ages and dies, even though that generation is having smaller families than their parents had. An uneven age composition, in which the childbearing generation is much larger than the elderly generation, produces population growth even though fertility is low by historical standards. Indeed, in 1992, the United States grew by more than 2.0 million people from natural increase alone, despite a TFR below replacement level. Significant levels of net migration into a country can further delay the achievement of zero population growth.

A country with an even age composition is illustrated by the population pyramid for country C, where fertility is low and mortality has similarly been constant. All the age groups are about the same size, and the number of births is very close to the number of deaths. Several European countries have population pyramids that resemble country C's.

Exercise

Based on the most recent Population Reference Bureau World Population Data Sheet, find the following figures. Compare them with those given in the text for 1992. Have basic demographic facts changed significantly since 1992? Can you speculate on why or why not?

1. The world's population

2. World natural increase

3. World doubling time

4. Natural increase and doubling time for developed countries

5. Natural increase and doubling time for developing countries, with and without China

6. The world's fastest-growing country in percentage terms

7. The country with the world's lowest growth rate

8. The population of the United States

9. Natural increase and doubling time of the United States

10. Absolute increase in the U.S. population from natural increase

11. Highest and lowest infant mortality rates in the world

* * *

The five elements of demography discussed in this section—growth rates, fertility, mortality, zero population growth, and population structure—are essential to an understanding of the future of world population and its likely interaction with global environmental change. Also required is an understanding of the patterns of growth around the world today, which are addressed in the next section.

II

Patterns of Population Growth and Fertility

The entire world's population, which exceeded 5.4 billion in 1992, is growing at about 1.7% a year. That means a doubling time slightly longer than 41 years, if that growth rate does not slow. This rate is down from a peak of about 2% during the sixties; since then, birth rates have declined in all parts of the world except Africa and the Middle East.

Despite slower growth in the world's population, more people are added to the total now than ever before because of the larger population base. The difference of course is between a *rate* of growth and growth in *absolute numbers*.

In 1992, the world's population grew by about 92 million people. Of that number, 94% lived in Africa, Asia, and Latin America, with Asia alone contributing 63% of the total. Natural increase in the United States contributed over a third of the remaining 6.0%.

It is possible to look at the geographic pattern of population growth in greater detail. Japan, Russia, Ukraine, Belarus, and most of Europe, which together made up 13% of the world's population in 1992, were close to zero population growth in that year, with rates of natural increase at or below 0.3%. Even so, their contribution to the increase in world population was 1.2 million, or just over 1% of the total. One fourth of this increase was in Russia.

Another 8.4% of the world's population was experiencing relatively slow but still substantial annual rates of natural increase—from 0.4% to 0.9%. Those countries included the United States, France, Poland, Canada, Australia, and the Netherlands. The United States made up more than half the population of this group and

contributed almost two-thirds of the nearly 3.2 million annual increase in population.

A third of the world's population is growing between 1.0% and 1.9% a year, a significant rate of increase, especially considering the large size of some members of this group. China, a fifth of the world's population by itself, dominates it, but it also includes Indonesia, Brazil, Thailand, South Korea, and Myanmar. Together, these countries contributed 28% of the 92-million-person increase in world population in 1992; China alone contributed more than 15 million additional people.

Another third of the world's population is growing at rates between 2.0% and 2.9% a year. These are very rapid rates that, without abatement, translate into doubling times of between 24 and 35 years. India, with nearly 900 million people, dominates this group, but several other giants are included as well: Bangladesh, Mexico, Vietnam, the Philippines, Turkey, Ethiopia, and Egypt. These countries contribute disproportionately to world population growth: 42% of the total increase in 1992.

A final 12% of global population is growing extraordinarily fast, at natural increase rates of 3.0% or more. Pakistan is the largest country in this group, and its growth rate means that, alone, it contributed nearly 3.8 million additional people to the world's population in 1992. Other large countries, both in population size and annual increase, include Nigeria, Iran, and Zaire. Together, the countries in this group contributed nearly a fourth of the world's total 1992 population growth.

The 17 countries that contributed a million or more people to the world's population in

1992 are listed in Table 1 in order of their contribution. Together, they accounted for more than two-thirds of the total increase. If the countries of the former Soviet Union are aggregated, they contributed nearly another 2 million people to the world's population. Europe as a whole added just over 1 million.

The pattern of fertility around the world today bears considerable resemblance to the pattern of population growth, but the match isn't perfect. While any cutoff is a bit arbitrary, and the credibility and precision of data on fertility rates vary from place to place, it is useful to divide the countries of the world into the following groups:

1. Countries with TFRs at or below replacement level (2.1 children per woman in this discussion);

2. Those with TFRs above replacement but not as high as a three-child norm (TFR 2.2–2.9);

3. Countries with medium to high fertility rates (TFR 3.0–3.9);

4. Countries with high to very high fertility rates (TFR 4.0 and above).

Table 2 summarizes the total population and the percentage of the world's population in each category. As that table shows, approximately one-fourth of the world's population is in each group.

More specifically, about 1.2 billion people live in countries with fertility at or below replacement level. This group includes most of Europe, the European portions of the former Soviet Union, Canada, the United States, Australia, New Zealand, Japan, South Korea, and some Asian island states such as Singapore and Hong Kong—the industrialized, and usually wealthy, countries of the world. This low-fertility group does not correspond precisely with the lowest-growth group, because an uneven age structure keeps some of these countries growing.

Another 1.4 billion people live where fertility exceeds replacement but does not reach three children per woman. China dominates this group, which also includes Thailand, North Korea, Sri Lanka, Colombia, Argentina, Iceland, Ireland, and five former Soviet republics.

Almost 1.5 billion people live in countries where fertility is between 3.0 and 3.9 children per woman. These include India, Indonesia, Malaysia, and Myanmar in Asia; Costa Rica, Mexico, Brazil, Ecuador, and Venezuela in Latin America; Turkey, Tunisia, and Lebanon in southwest Asia; and Kyrgyzstan of the former Soviet Union.

Nearly 1.3 billion people live in countries where families have an average of four or more children. Included in this group are nearly all the countries on the continent of Africa and in the Middle East; Afghanistan and Iran; Nepal, Pakistan, and Bangladesh; Laos, Cambodia,

Table 1 Countries Contributing 1 Million or More to World Population in 1992	
Country	**Contribution (in millions)**
India	17.65
China	15.16
Pakistan	3.77
Indonesia	3.14
Brazil	2.87
Nigeria	2.70
Bangladesh	2.67
United States	2.04
Mexico	2.02
Iran	1.97
Philippines	1.53
Ethiopia	1.52
Vietnam	1.52
Egypt	1.34
Turkey	1.30
Zaire	1.17
South Africa	1.08

Source: Population Reference Bureau, 1992 World Population Data Sheet

Vietnam, and the Philippines; all of Central America but Costa Rica, Mexico, and Panama; Peru, Bolivia, and Paraguay; and three former Soviet republics in central Asia. Two-thirds of the 1.3 billion people live in countries where families average five or more children.

Another dominant feature of fertility patterns is their decline in many countries in the past three decades. Birth rates have fallen very rapidly in some parts of the world and by at least a third in some 26 countries. In Singapore, Hong Kong, and Taiwan, for example, total fertility rates have fallen by at least 70%, from more than six to fewer than two children per woman. In four other countries (China, Cuba, Mauritius, and Thailand), TFRs have fallen by about two-thirds, to levels close to but above replacement. In several other countries, women have around half as many children as their mothers and aunts had 30 years ago. Mexico, Brazil, Colombia, Costa Rica, Turkey, Venezuela, and the United States are in that category. In India, the Philippines, Egypt, and Peru, fertility has fallen by about a third.

Exercises

1. Using the Population Reference Bureau Data Sheet, make a table of the percentage of married women using modern contraception in

Table 2
1992 Population and Percentage of World Population by Total Fertility Rate (TFR)

TFR	Total Population (in billions)	% of World Population
≤ 2.1	1.2	23
2.2–2.9	1.4	26
3.0–3.9	1.5	27
≥ 4.0	1.3	24

Source: Population Reference Bureau, *1992 World Population Data Sheet*

each of the categories of total fertility rates used in this text (at or below replacement level; 2.2–2.9; 3.0–3.9; 4.0 and above) for countries with populations of more than one million (where data are available). What conclusions can you draw?

2. Plot on a graph the relationship between total fertility rate and gross national product per capita for countries with populations of more than 1 million from the data sheet (except include all the countries of Western Asia for which data are available regardless of population size). What conclusions can you draw?

Discussion

1. The following conclusions are based on 1992 data; your results may differ. It is perhaps not surprising that where fertility is lower, use of modern family planning methods is more widespread—in general. Modern family planning methods (the pill, condom, IUD, and sterilization; see the definitions on the back of the data sheet) are used by between 60% and 75% of married women of reproductive age in the countries where fertility is at or below replacement level, except in Italy, Portugal, Spain, Eastern Europe, and the European republics of the former Soviet Union. (In all but the former Soviet republics, similarly high percentages of fertile, married women use some form of contraception, but more than half use traditional methods that include coitus interruptus—withdrawal before ejaculation—and rhythm). In the Belarus, Russia, and the Ukraine, data on traditional methods do not exist, and less than a quarter of married women of reproductive age use modern methods. (It is widely understood that abortion is responsible for the low birth rates in those countries where modern contraception is not widely used.)

Where fertility exceeds replacement level but does not reach the three-child norm, and where data are available, 40% to 55% of women of reproductive age use modern contraception. Use rates are higher in Thailand and Puerto Rico, where nearly two-thirds of married women use modern contraception, and in China, where 70% do. And use rates are lower in the former Soviet republics: less than a tenth to a fifth of married women. (Again, abortion is responsible for the lower-than-expected fertilities in the former Soviet republics.)

Where fertility is between 3.0 and 3.9 children per woman, between a third and half of them use modern contraception. In countries where families have on average between four and five children, use of modern contraceptives runs from about a quarter to less than half of couples. In the highest-fertility countries, many use rates run in the single digits, with most of the rest lying between 10% and 25%. Zimbabwe and Honduras are exceptions, with approximately a third of couples using modern contraception.

While in general fertility goes down as use of modern contraception goes up, the relationship is far from perfect. For example, China and Thailand have total fertility rates—2.2 and 2.4, respectively—a bit higher than one would expect from their use of modern contraception: 70% in China and 64% in Thailand. Elsewhere in the world (for example in Switzerland, Norway, and the United Kingdom), contraceptive prevalence that high is associated with lower fertility. Similarly, Zimbabwe has a TFR of 5.6 with, if the numbers are reliable, 36% of women of reproductive age using modern contraceptives; Spain—again, if the numbers are credible—achieves a total fertility rate of 1.3 with 38% use of modern contraceptives.

Culture may explain why a very high use of modern contraception in China still yields a fertility of 2.2. The Chinese have a long tradition of large families, including a strong preference for sons, a tradition that is only partially overtaken by strong government policy in favor of small families. Likewise in Zimbabwe: couples may be using modern contraception there to space the five or six children they want to have, rather than to limit themselves to the three or four children one might expect from that level of contraceptive use.

2. Conventional wisdom holds that the strongest explanation of fertility lies with wealth—that as people become richer, they have fewer children. Again, this has a general truth to it, but it is not uniformly the case. The countries with the lowest fertility in 1992 do include the wealthiest—Japan and the countries of Europe and North America, with gross national products per capita of $15,000 to more than $30,000. Likewise, the highest-fertility countries are in general the poorest—most of Africa, Bangladesh, Nepal, southeast Asian countries with a recent history of war (Vietnam, Cambodia, and Laos), and some of the poorest countries of Latin America, such as El Salvador, Guatemala, Nicaragua, Bolivia, and Peru.

On the other hand, Middle Eastern oil-exporting countries with per capita GNPs of nearly $20,000, comparable to those in Europe and North America, have fertilities among the highest in the world. Among the rest of the high-fertility group, GNPs per capita vary from below $200 to $3,000; and included in the low-fertility countries are Greece, Portugal, South Korea, and some former Eastern Bloc countries, with per capita GNPs between $2,000 and $6,000. So the match between high income and low fertility is far from perfect.

III

Determinants of Fertility

Fertility is the driving force of population growth in the world today. Mortality rates are relatively low around the world by historical standards, though exceptions exist. Reductions in infant and maternal deaths, universally hailed as desirable, would increase population growth little compared with how powerfully reductions in fertility could curb it.

Fertility is the logical target for reducing population growth because of the place we occupy today in the history of population change. It is widely believed that for most of human history fertility and mortality were both quite high and kept human populations from growing except very slowly over very long time scales. Population growth "took off" on its dramatic rise when death rates started to fall with the advent of industrialization and, even more importantly, the development of the germ theory of disease, healthy sanitation practices, and antibiotics and other medicines. This decline in mortality began in the industrialized world in the nineteenth century and spread to the Third World after World War II, making relatively low death rates virtually a worldwide phenomenon.

In some countries fertility has followed mortality in its decline. Births and deaths are in another equilibrium, producing slow or no growth, but this time at lower levels. These are the countries that are close to zero population growth. Elsewhere, of course, fertility has not fallen to match mortality. Indeed, the essence of rapid world population growth today is this incongruence between fertility and mortality rates. The gap is greatest in the countries where population growth is most rapid, where fertility is at a peak or has just begun to fall. Growth rates are slower where the decline in fertility has been under way for a longer time or has been more rapid. Where growth rates are nearly zero, the transition to a low-fertility regime is nearly complete.

What drives variations in fertility such as those that are observable in the long sweep of human population history and in the pattern of fertility around the world? It is usual to consider the determinants of fertility in two classes—proximate, or immediate determinants, and social and economic conditions that affect fertility.

A discussion of the proximate determinants of fertility is best undertaken in the context of a question that seems paradoxical in a world where high fertility is considered a problem. That question is not why fertility is so high, but why it is not higher. Demographers estimate that, as a matter of physical possibility, the average woman is capable of bearing 17 children in a reproductive lifetime stretching from age 15 to age 50. Of course, this level is only occasionally achieved by individual women, and on a country-wide basis does not occur in the world today even in the highest-fertility countries. So what prevents humans from reaching this theoretical maximum?

In some cases biological conditions reduce fertility. Some portion of any population is sterile, and another portion is subfecund, or less fertile than it would be, because of malnutrition or disease, especially sexually transmitted disease. Even among fully fertile people, in most countries in the world today, women marry some years after age 15 or the onset of fertility, so that age at first marriage is a significant determinant of fertility. Marriage at 20 avoids three births; in Sri Lanka, age at marriage is estimated to avoid five births for the average woman.

Another limit on fertility is of primarily historical importance: widespread celibacy. For several centuries in Europe before the development of industrial society, fertility was lower than is usual in societies that are not using modern contraceptives. In mid-nineteenth-century Belgium, for example, 15% of women and 18% of men never married. Many of those who remained celibate were lifelong servants in the houses of others. In Ireland, it is suggested that severe economic conditions contributed to celibacy. The incidence of celibacy around the world today, however, is not large enough to affect fertility significantly.

Breast-feeding, which usually suppresses ovulation, is a natural contraceptive. Where it is practiced for two years or more, it can further reduce the actual number of births from the theoretical maximum. In Bangladesh, where the average mother breast-feeds each of her children for 29 months, the practice is estimated to reduce the average Bangladeshi woman's total births by nearly seven. In some cultures, breast-feeding's effect on fertility is intensified by a taboo on postpartum intercourse. In Africa and South Asia, this taboo has been of historical and local significance. It is widely thought that modernization, including urbanization, is undermining this practice today.

The fertility-reduction practice most familiar to Americans is contraception. Precursors of modern condoms and diaphragms were used to avoid conception in ancient Egypt and classical Greece and Rome. Most cultures contain some folk wisdom, always for women, about avoiding conception, such as herbal concoctions for drinking or applying locally and behaviors such as jumping over sticks or otherwise exerting oneself after intercourse. Coitus interruptus, an ancient method still in widespread use today, requires male initiative. Other traditional methods include abstinence and rhythm.

Modern methods of contraception include the oral contraceptive pill; hormonal injections or implants; the intrauterine device, or IUD; barrier methods such as condoms, diaphragms, and sponges, often used with chemical spermicides; and surgical sterilization. Abortion is not technically a method of contraception, but it plays an important role around the world in preventing births.

Broader social, cultural, and economic conditions also influence fertility levels. High fertility is usually found in countries where poverty is widespread and deep. Where women do not often work for significant wages, bearing and raising children is easily integrated into their traditional unpaid work: producing, processing, and preparing food, gathering fuel and water, and other work in and near the home. The wages for women who work outside the home in these countries are always low; a mother can take time out for childbirth without sacrificing much pay, and another child can in just a few years easily make up such a minor loss with its own labor. The need for child labor also drives fertility up, especially in agricultural communities but also anywhere that families rely on the physical environment for subsistence, as for gathering wood for fuel and drawing water. A lack of schooling opportunities reinforces this effect. Another important condition of high fertility is a culture in which women have little or no prestige except that gained by bearing children, especially sons. A preference for sons also increases fertility, as couples keep having children until they achieve the number of sons that they want. High rates of infant and child mortality have the same effect. Finally, in societies without public old-age pensions, children represent the only opportunity a couple has for support in old age.

Wealthy, industrialized societies, where women increasingly compete as near-equals to men in the workplace, have the opposite conditions, conditions that encourage low fertility. Taking time off from work to bear and raise children represents a major loss in a society where women are significant wage earners and where they usually have sources of prestige other than multiple child bearing. The sheer cost of raising a child in a complex technological society, where mass consumption is the rule and a college education is desirable, can be a deterrent as well. Child labor is illegal in most wealthy, industrialized countries, and compulsory schooling until at least age 16 is the norm, reinforcing the high cost of having children. Preference for males is not as marked as in the poorer countries, and infant and child mortality rates are low. Finally, widespread old-age pensions and a weakening of the sense of obligation that adult children have to support their parents combine to remove security in old age as a spur to repeated child bearing.

Thus a complex constellation of factors affects fertility, from basic health to contraceptive use to the status of women. If a government is interested in encouraging a reduction in fertility, it must affect one or more of these determinants. In a time of constrained budgets nearly everywhere, how is a government to know which of the many factors is most important or will work most effectively? Recent analyses of the declines in fertility of the past 30 years provide an answer.

Analysts of these declines and of the pattern of fertility around the world in general have begun to converge on a few relatively simple ideas that explain most of the variation in fertility. First in importance is the status of women. Second is primary health care, particularly health care that keeps infants and children alive and improves the health of mothers. The final element is a family planning program that offers a full range of contraceptive options and is supported by rhetoric from the highest level of government.

In general, fertility is highest where women's status is lowest. Africa, the Arab states, and portions of South Asia have the world's highest fertility rates. And by measures such as education, health, and income, their women have low status. In places where fertility has fallen, women have options other than motherhood from which to gain prestige and a place in their culture. The importance of the status of women to fertility is reflected in the focus of the U.N.'s International Conference on Population and Development, held in Cairo, Egypt, in September 1994, on what it called the "empowerment of women" as both an end in itself and as a means to reduce fertility.

Fertility is also higher where infant and child mortality are high. It is not hard to understand the motivation of parents who keep bearing children, in fear that some of them will die in childhood, in order to achieve the family size that they really want. Where primary health care keeps babies alive, fertility is lower.

Finally, successful family planning programs are associated with lower fertility around the world. These programs succeed in bringing about a fall in fertility when they are designed with sensitivity to the culture in which they are offered and carried out by local people. Programs also succeed that provide the full range of contraceptive options, from condoms to sterilization, to all people. And programs succeed the most when they are coupled with strong rhetorical support from the government—statements that make having smaller families a patriotic act.

Family planning programs work not only to reduce fertility directly but also to improve infant and maternal health. Where fertility is high, women must have early, late, and closely spaced pregnancies. All of these are high-risk. Family planning allows women to delay and space pregnancies, and prevent high-risk pregnancies; thus it can work as an element of primary health care, in addition to reducing fertility. In so doing, it is preparing the ground for its own further acceptance.

Thus the job of bringing fertility down to the replacement levels required to stabilize world population is somewhat simplified. A precise kind of development is called for that raises the status of women by widening opportunities for education and work, as well as according more legal rights; brings primary health care to all with a particular emphasis on improving infant and child health; and makes the full range of family planning services available everywhere.

This approach to halting world population growth promises to be more effective than the approach envisioned by the traditionally dominant theory of population change, the **demographic transition theory**. We described trends in fertility and mortality over the long sweep of history at the beginning of this section. For most of history, both fertility and mortality were high and balanced, resulting in slow growth, if any. Then, with industrialization, higher incomes, and the introduction of modern medicine, mortality fell dramatically in Europe and North America. Fertility at first stayed high, resulting in very rapid rates of population growth. Then fertility fell to match mortality again, resulting in slow growth at lower levels of fertility and mortality. This three-part sequence makes up the demographic transition theory.

The theory holds that as a country becomes wealthy and industrialized, fertility will fall automatically. As it happened in Europe and North America, the theory goes, so it can happen in the now rapidly growing Third World, if only people can become prosperous enough.

Increasingly, however, dissenting voices have questioned the validity of the demographic transition theory. Some have argued that waiting until the Third World is wealthy for population to stabilize means that the ultimate size of the world's population will be too great to avoid harm from environmental problems and resource scarcities. Others have said that the rapid population growth now characteristic of the Third World precludes the kind of large-scale and widespread economic development required to reduce fertility and slow population growth. The notion here is that some high-fertility Third World countries are trapped in the second stage of the demographic transition theory and cannot break loose without some kind of intervention.

Recognizing the importance of the status of women, maternal and child health, and family planning to fertility and population stabilization sidesteps some of the conundrums of the demographic transition theory. Instead of assuming that wealth created by industrialization will eventually trickle down to women and children, economic development should be targeted specifically at raising women's status, improving maternal and child health, and bringing family planning to all couples. In the current less-than-generous economic age, this is a least-cost strategy. It can solve immediate problems while simultaneously creating conditions that increase the likelihood of further growth in wealth and well-being in the future by improving the wealth and well-being of the building blocks of economies, individual people.

Exercise

Using the data sheet, plot infant mortality against total fertility rate for the countries of the world with populations of one million or more. Formulate a hypothesis about the relationship between infant mortality and fertility.

IV
Policies for Encouraging Smaller Families

Given what is known about the determinants of fertility, a government that is interested in lowering fertility in its country has a number of options. Through legislation, commitment of funds, and public statements, a government can affect the availability of family planning and primary health care services; the range of contraceptives available in the country; public education for family planning; marriage age; schooling opportunities, especially for girls; legal status of women; work opportunities for women; and other aspects of women's status.

The discussion that follows is intended to apply to a developing country with relatively high fertility and low status of women, where not everyone has ready access to health care, either privately or publicly provided. It is assumed that not all children are in school, either at the primary or the secondary level. It is further assumed that incomes are quite low and that a significant portion of the country is rural and agricultural.

The government would want a complete supply of the full range of contraceptives available for everyone wanting them. It should lift any trade barriers or bans on the import of particular contraceptive commodities and encourage the domestic manufacture of contraceptives. If budgets allowed, it might want to support research into new contraceptives. Legal restrictions on the use of contraceptives would need to be lifted. A government interested in the *fullest* range of family planning services would ensure that abortion is legal and readily available. It is widely agreed that achieving replacement-level fertility with current contraceptive technologies—and human nature—is not possible without the option of abortion. Of course, abortion raises religious and moral questions that not all countries answer permissively.

Also important are doctors, nurses, and other health professionals trained in family planning. A government can subsidize medical training, either at home or abroad, and encourage or require the inclusion of family planning in such training.

In addition to the sheer legal availability of contraceptives and abortion, the government would want to ensure that family planning services are actually available to everyone regardless of income or geographic location. Thus it might want to fund public family planning clinics, including mobile units to reach even the remotest areas.

An enormously effective and inexpensive method of public education in family planning takes very little effort on the part of a government: announcements and other public messages that having fewer children is the *right* thing to do now, amounting to a patriotic act. A government can also encourage the promulgation of similar messages, as well as practical information about locations of clinics and availability of services, in the media.

Family planning services are best offered in the larger context of primary health care, particularly maternal and child health care. In a very poor country, where the status of women is low, having many children makes economic and cultural sense, and many children die in infancy. At best, offering family planning services in isolation, apart from other health care, may simply elicit no interest. At worst, it may seem a cruel joke to parents struggling to keep children alive. Within a system of primary health care, too, it makes sense—both from the point of view of population stabilization and for humanitarian reasons—to encourage breast-feeding and to focus on the package of immunization, nutrition, and sanitation practices that contribute to keeping infants and children alive.

A government can pass laws raising the legal age at first marriage, which may technically hold hope of reducing fertility. A law alone, however, may change nothing about marriage practices without accompanying public education and efforts to change cultural habits. Cultural changes such as these usually take more than the passage of a law.

Moving toward universal enrollment of both boys and girls in primary and secondary school works on several levels to encourage lower fertility. Better educated people are open to new ideas and can take better advantage of work opportunities. Education specifically on family planning and health care for infants and children can lead directly to lower fertility and smaller, healthier families. Every year that a girl stays in school usually reduces the ultimate size of her future family. Keeping girls in school also improves their chances for well-paid employment, participation in public life, self-determination, and other indicators of higher status.

A large package of legal and other reforms beyond education is needed to raise the status of women more broadly in a society. For example, women need the right to own and inherit property and to borrow money to have the fullest range of economic opportunities; in many countries, women do not have these rights. Marriage may disadvantage women by putting all family property in the husband's name or by making it easier for men to divorce their wives than it is for women to divorce their husbands, and then requiring no child support or alimony. In many countries, too, the notion of equal pay for equal work is a foreign one; women receive lower wages than men, whether it is for equal work or not. Another area of law

relating to the status of women involves domestic violence. The status of women can never be truly equal to that of men, or even higher than it is today, if women are at risk of injury and even death in their own homes. Thus laws and customs that overlook domestic violence, that make it nearly impossible for women to be protected from violence at the hands of their husbands, and that leave domestic violence unpunished all contribute to the low status of women and, directly and indirectly, to higher fertility.

A government interested in raising the status of women would look beyond strict legalities and develop programs to complement the kinds of changes mentioned above. For example, in addition to enacting laws requiring equal pay for equal work or nondiscrimination in the workplace, a government could fund programs that provide credit to women to begin small businesses—indeed, in many Third World countries today, programs that make "micro-loans" to women already enjoy considerable success. A government could institute programs to train women for a wider range of work. It could also fund private groups working to improve women's lives, from groups that deal with domestic violence to those that provide health care and family planning.

A final area of interest to a government wishing to encourage a fertility decline involves incentives and disincentives in family planning programs. Incentives and disincentives are, generally, rewards and penalties designed to promote the use of contraception and the adoption of a small-family norm, or the replacement-level fertility required for population stabilization. They can be part of the administration of a family planning program, such as the payment of small sums to people who accept a family planning method or to doctors or family planning workers for recruiting acceptors. They can also be larger-scale efforts that link development projects for a community with the acceptance of family planning or the achievement of certain goals such as numbers of births. Or they can impose penalties on families that exceed a certain number of births.

The oldest and most common incentive is a small one-time payment or in-kind contribution (such as a clean garment) to a person who accepts a family planning method, usually sterilization. First used in India in the 1950s, this kind of incentive is offered in some two dozen countries around the world. Experience shows that offering incentives can in fact increase the number of acceptors of sterilization.

In most cases, a payment is intended to compensate the acceptor for lost wages, the costs of travel, and meals involved in coming to a family planning clinic to be sterilized. In fact, however, even small payments can act as an inducement, especially in very poor countries. Some critics of these incentives argue that the risk of coercion is so great that they should be eliminated, especially for sterilization, a permanent and surgical method of birth control. Coercion occurs when an incentive is so attractive to a person that it exerts what is called in law **undue influence** on a person's decision; that is, voluntary, informed consent becomes impossible because the extreme attractiveness of the incentive is substituted for true weighing of alternatives. Others argue that well-designed programs, with counseling and payments matched to actual costs incurred, can insure informed consent in family planning programs.

Two other kinds of incentive schemes attempt to improve people's lives significantly by changing the circumstances that lead them to have many children. They are deferred incentive schemes and community development incentives. Deferred incentive schemes involve periodic payments to an account or fund for people who limit their families. The idea is to substitute future payments for the security that children bring. Payments can take the form of old-age pensions, life insurance, education funds, and the like, and are collected in the future, when people have succeeded in having a small family. Deferred incentive schemes leave the choice of birth control method to the individual and reward behavior over a long period of time that requires deliberate thought. This avoids the last-minute pressure and risk of undue influence that can be present in one-time payment schemes.

A number of imaginative deferred incentive schemes have been devised; a few of these have been tried in pilot programs in Taiwan and India, with some success in reducing fertility. The problem is that to have a national effect on birth rates the program would have to be national in scope and would thus cost a great deal of money; indeed, it would amount to nothing short of a national social security or social welfare program. Finally, for such a program to work, a national government needs to have meaningful contact with its citizens, who in turn have confidence in the solvency and good faith of their government. Such is not the rule in many poor countries in the world today.

Community development incentives have most of the advantages of deferred payment programs and few of the disadvantages. The government agrees to reward a community with a project that will increase its wealth. This might be a well, irrigation, a diesel pump, livestock, a biogas plant, a school, roads, parasite control, or low-interest loans. The projects are funded as the community complies with specified family planning or fertility goals, such as contraception practiced by 60% of couples, or fertility not exceeding an average of two or three children per family. The programs are sometimes quite complex, involving deferred payments and participation by individuals earning shares in a common fund. Thailand and Indonesia have community development projects linked to family planning and have seen some local successes. Such programs can be carried out locally and enforced through local mechanisms, avoiding the problem of lack of contact and confidence that national governments can experience with villages in poor countries. On the other hand, a successful community project requires social cohesion in villages, which does not exist everywhere. And these programs rely on local peer pressure, which can come from elites and be the most direct kind of coercion.

Disincentives are the other side of the coin from incentives; these measures impose costs on large families or withhold benefits such as housing subsidies, employment benefits, or preference in school admission. Singapore has the longest experience with disincentives, and China has disincentive policies in place in some regions. Disincentives are not widely used, in part because few countries wealthy enough for them to be meaningful have population policies that limit family size. And Singapore has in recent years moved away from its low fertility policies and is attempting to encourage births, without significant success.

Disincentives are economical; they deprive people of things that would otherwise cost the government money. But they have their share of drawbacks. A disincentive can impose a cost so high, or deprive an individual of something so fundamentally necessary, that it amounts to coercion. Withholding food from the poor if they have many children, for example, is so punitive that it becomes pure compulsion. If not fashioned carefully, too, disincentives can punish the innocent. It can be argued that denying children admission to the best schools because they come from a large family punishes them for their parents' acts.

All incentives and disincentives involving family planning have advantages and disadvantages. In any given country, whether the good aspects outweigh the bad depends on the particular circumstances. Whatever else is true of incentives and disincentives, they are not the first or the only step a government or family planning program should take to curb population growth. Indeed, without a larger context of improving the health of mothers and babies, raising the status of women, and offering the full range of family planning services to everyone, incentives and disincentives have very little chance of affecting fertility behavior and have a very great chance of doing violence to an individual's bodily integrity and free choice.

Exercises

1. This section spoke exclusively about the kinds of policies that the government of a Third World country could consider adopting to reduce fertility and slow population growth in its own country. As U.S. residents our perspective is usually a different one: how the United States, through financial assistance to developing countries, can affect fertility and population growth in those countries. Make a list of policies, parallel to the ones discussed in the text, that the United States might promote in developing countries through financial assistance. What is acceptable, in your view, for this country to promote in others? Are some things unacceptable? Does the United States have an obligation to promote or support certain activities in other countries, in your view?

2. Also of relevance to world population growth and to issues of domestic and international population policy is the policy of the United States towards its own fertility rates and population growth. What kinds of policies affect fertility and population growth in a wealthy country like the United States? What sorts of policies would you find most acceptable? Which most unacceptable? Why?

V

The Future of World Population

In preceding sections, we have mentioned that the world's population in 1992 was growing at a rate that would allow the number of people in the world to double in 41 years. If that rate of growth indeed continued unabated, the world's population would reach nearly 1.4 trillion in the year 2320, after eight doublings. This calculation is offered more for its shock value than for its predictive value. Indeed, it illustrates the power of exponential growth and short doubling times, not the most likely future path of human population growth. Many say that it illustrates the impossibility of population growth continuing without cease.

As we know, in the past three decades fertility has fallen in most regions of the world except Africa and the Middle East. The conditions that accompanied that decline and the changes required to duplicate them elsewhere are also understood. We know too that mortality rates have fallen all over the world. The conditions that accompany different death rates are similarly well understood. Given all this, it is possible to project future world population size, based on estimates of future fertility and mortality and the growth already built in with existing populations. (See the system modeling module to build a simple model of human population.)

Projections should always be distinguished from forecasts. Population projections are always exercises that yield a result of a certain character: an illustration of what the future would be *if certain assumptions turn out to be true and nothing else happens to contradict or overcome those assumptions.* Projections depend for their validity as much on the validity of the assumptions as on their mathematical correctness. A population projection is a mathematical exercise illustrating the results of particular combinations of fertility and mortality regimes. It is not a prediction that certain fertility and mortality regimes will in fact occur, though modelers usually choose fertility and mortality regimes that are reasonable, and even likely. Sets of projections are also useful for comparing the likely demographic results of differing policies affecting fertility and mortality, within the context of the models' assumptions.

Given this understanding of population projections, it is useful to study the most recent set of projections of world population carried out by the United Nations, in 1990. As is their custom, the U.N. group ran three model projections, labeled "high," "medium," and "low" for the differing fertility reduction paths that they assumed. (All three projections assumed the same mortality pattern.)

The medium projection is considered by U.N. demographers to be the most probable. It assumes that family size in the Third World outside China will fall gradually from its current level of 4.4 children to 3.3 by the year 2000 and to replacement level fertility between 35 and 55 years from now. Average world fertility would then be at approximately replacement level. Given this change in fertility, world population rises from its current level of over 5 billion to 10 billion in 2050 and then stabilizes at 11.6 billion in 2150.

The medium projection assumes that fertility will fall to replacement level around the world and no lower. We know, however, that fertility has fallen below two children per woman in many places in the world, not all of them industrialized. The notion that average world fertility could fall to 1.7 underlies the low projection, in which world population peaks at about 8 billion in 2050 and then declines gradually thereafter, dropping below today's population in approximately 2100.

The low projection stretches the imagination. Realizing it would require the most optimistic vision of future maternal, infant, and child health; status of women; family planning programs; and sustainable development. In contrast, the high projection is based on slower progress on these fronts than either of the others—though progress is still required. The high projection assumes that it would take ten years more than in the medium projection for fertility in the Third World to reach 3.3. Then it would fall not to replacement level but just above it, to 2.2 children per woman. This set of assumptions about fertility produces a projected world population of 12.5 billion in 2050 and of more than 20 billion a century later, with no prospect of stabilization in sight.

Each of these three projections starts at the same point, with world population as it is today. And 2.5 to 3.0 billion additional people are virtually assured, even if fertility were to fall immediately to replacement level everywhere in the world, because of the large generation of children now living who have yet to reach their childbearing years. Beyond this certainty, the scale of additional growth in the world's population depends on what actions are taken to reduce fertility—and how fast they are taken. A delay of 10 years in reaching an average Third World fertility of 3.3 between the medium and high projections produces 2.5 billion more people in 2050, as many people as the entire world had in 1950. A century later, the difference between the high and medium projections is more than 9 billion people, nearly twice today's world population.

Thus actions taken now, then augmented and repeated over the coming decades, could reduce the eventual population of the world by nearly twice as many people as inhabit the Earth today. Not taking those actions could increase it by as much. Figure 4

illustrates the three U.N. projections.

How likely in fact is the U.N.'s medium projection? It is a rule of thumb that when roughly 70% of married women of reproductive age use modern contraception, fertility approximates two children per woman. Modern contraception is used by as few as 1% or 2% of women of reproductive age in the highest fertility countries around the world, especially in Africa and the Middle East. Elsewhere in the Third World, 70% use of modern contraceptives is rare. In fact, in the developing world as a whole outside China, an average of 43% of childbearing women use modern contraceptives. How likely is it, then, that usage rates will reach 70%?

Some data derived from surveys give clues to the answer to this question. The United Nations estimates that one in five pregnancies in the world today is unwanted. It has also calculated that if all Third World women who say in response to survey questions that they want no more children were able to stop having them, the number of births would fall by between 27% and 35%. That would bring the average number of children per woman from 6.1 to 4.4

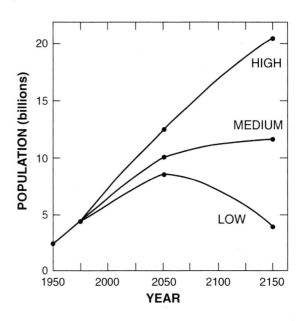

Figure 4. U.N. high, medium, and low variant projections of world population to 2150. Source: United Nations Population Fund.

in Africa; from 3.9 to 2.6 in Asia; and from 3.4 to 2.2 in Latin America. In Africa, for example, 77% of married women who want no more children are not using contraceptives. Furthermore, the United Nations has found that nearly nine out of ten women surveyed would have preferred to space their births two years apart or more, but only six out of ten managed to do so. Nearly half of them said they would prefer intervals between births of four years or more, though only 16% actually achieved it. All of these facts represent significant unmet demand for family planning services. Moving beyond this currently unmet demand to 70% of couples using modern contraceptives would require changes in the conditions that encourage repeated childbearing.

A group in Washington, D.C., Population Action International, has calculated the cost of supplying the family planning services required to achieve 70% modern contraceptive use. They estimate that it costs roughly $16 to provide family planning to a couple for a year—just contraceptives, not other health care, not education for women and girls, not employment opportunities for women. This means a total annual investment in family planning alone of $10.5 billion. This is roughly three times the total current investment in family planning, but a tiny proportion of total world expenditures on other matters.

At the beginning of this section, the point was made that if the current rate of world population growth did not abate, the world's population would continue doubling without cease, reaching 1.4 trillion in 2320, and doubling again by 2361 to 2.8 trillion. The point was also made that almost no one expects such growth to occur. Either they see fertility declining now, with additional efforts in place or being suggested to accelerate these declines and spread them geographically, or they believe that the world is simply not likely to support, either physically or socially, human populations of trillions of people.

Many analysts who study world population growth and consider it a problem say that if

human beings do not themselves curb their growth in numbers, by reducing birth rates, then "nature will do it for them" by increasing death rates through famine, disease, and—though it is not "natural" in the usual sense—war. These analysts usually rely on a biological model of human populations, arguing from predator-prey or population-food supply relations in the wild.

It is well understood that in a given geographical area, food supply for any animal population will limit that population to what is often called the area's **carrying capacity**. When the population of an animal grows beyond its food supply, or exceeds the area's carrying capacity, deaths will increase, or a population crash will occur, after which the balance between number of animals and supply of food is restored. This principle is then applied to human populations. It is said that if human populations exceed the globe's—or a particular region's—carrying capacity, a population crash or **dieback** will occur, with human deaths on a large scale from starvation, disease, warfare, or some other catastrophe.

These analysts may be correct. Human populations are indeed degrading the physical world's systems; global change is part of this degradation. And modernization and economic development have not banished famines, epidemics, or wars from the human scene. But the history of world population alone does not readily allow the conclusion that the human population is likely to experience a catastrophe that reduces its numbers significantly, forcing population into balance with resources. Such a mortality crisis would require conditions significantly different from those that have prevailed in the historical era.

It is not possible to know in detail the course of human population growth before the emergence of written records relevant to demography, such as censuses, tax rolls, and marriage records. For earlier times, historical demographers and anthropologists piece together physical evidence such as numbers of rooms in dwellings and food-growing potential of croplands. Within the constraints of the data, and based on later rather than earlier times, we can infer that the history of human population growth is dominated by its tremendous power, especially on the global scale, to overcome the effects of famine, epidemics, and warfare, which have recurred often in human history.

Since 1 A.D., the upward trend of world population has been interrupted three times. That trend stagnated between 200 and 400 A.D., when the Roman and Chinese Han Empires collapsed; stagnated, then fell, between 1200 and 1400, years that included the Black Death and its accompanying horrors in Europe and the conquest of China by the Mongols; and stagnated between 1600 and 1650 when, it is hypothesized, a climatic event called the Little Ice Age depressed agricultural production and caused famine. Population losses were always more devastating at the local than at the global scale. From 1200–1400, for example, populations of areas that are now France, Turkey, and China fell by as much as a third, while the world's population simply failed to grow in the 13th century, then fell by only 2.7% through the 14th. And significant local losses may have no effect on global numbers if the absolute numbers are not large; depopulation of the Americas after contact with Europeans, absolutely devastating for indigenous Americans, occurred during a period of steady increase in the global population.

Over the last century, with conditions more like the ones under which we live today, we know many more details about the demographic consequences of famine, epidemics, and warfare, harrowing details of suffering and dislocation. Yet it is widely understood that even the catastrophes with the severest demographic consequences usually have only a fleeting and relatively modest effect on regional populations and virtually none on world population.

For example, a famine occurred in China between 1957 and 1961 that involved 25–30 million more deaths and 30–35 million fewer births than would have been expected under normal conditions, making it a disaster with some of the most severe demographic consequences in modern history. Those years without doubt involved a staggering degree of human suffering, suffering that the world shrinks from and seeks to avoid repeating. Yet the population of China made a relatively quick numerical recovery from this disaster. TFR, which had fallen from 6.4 in 1957 to 3.3 in 1961, by 1963 had reached 7.5 births per woman, a dramatic illustration of the "hyperfertility" that often follows a famine or other event that depresses birth rates. China soon made up for the delay in population growth occasioned by the famine. Thirty years later, it has grown rapidly enough to a large enough size to alarm its leaders into introducing the most stringent set of policies to encourage small families ever seen. And growth in world population did not register the events of 1957–61 in China.

Much the same can be said of the loss of human life associated with the two world wars, the influenza pandemic of 1918, the Ukrainian famine of the early 1930s, and the famines that have plagued Africa.

In today's world, many people see the AIDS epidemic as evidence that disease will bring human numbers into balance with resources. But even in central Africa, where infection rates are the highest in the world, and where the disease is wreaking havoc on entire countries, mathematical models suggest that AIDS, as destructive of families and societies as it is, depresses the growth rate of affected populations but does not produce zero or negative growth rates on a regional scale. The impact on world population is, in turn, not noticeable.

World population history suggests that famine, epidemics, and wars have not curbed world population growth or even slowed it for very long, particularly in the most recent past. Thus the notion that nature will in some way take care of too-rapid population growth, making human efforts to reduce fertility and stabilize population growth unnecessary, is not well founded—if the past is a reliable guide to the future. As with any forward-looking enterprise, the qualitative projections of future population contained in the last few paragraphs are as dependent on their assumptions as are mathematical projections. They would be invalid if AIDS, for example, were to become insect-borne or airborne, or if another fatal, easily transmitted disease were to develop; if severe drought on a global scale were to reduce global food supply significantly; if other natural systems, such as forests, grasslands, or fisheries, were to collapse on a global scale from overuse or contamination; or if large-scale nuclear war were to occur. In short, if any event dramatically unlike the conditions under which world population history has unfolded were to affect the ability of human beings to feed, shelter, and clothe themselves, then population collapse or dieback could occur.

It is worth considering other alternatives as well. For example, might human populations adapt, as they have in the past, to ever-less-generous and dignified ways of life, to material, emotional, and spiritual deprivation that is significant but not enough to kill outright? Might social systems become more controlling and authoritarian, so that scarce resources are distributed under tight control, environmental degradation is rigidly regulated, and life in general is less free?

Human populations at their most basic are biological organisms pursuing the physical objects of food, shelter, and clothing in the material world. But they are also made up of thinking and feeling people who are part of families and larger-scale societies and governments. Stresses from rapid population growth and enormous absolute numbers may tell in these nonmaterial features of human life, as well as in the more familiarly analyzed material aspects involving food and physical well-being. Indeed, they may tell sooner. Thus material deprivation is not the only indicator of a poverty related to too many people too soon; poverty in the emotional, social, and political realms may be another.

Exercises

1. What is your view of the likely future of world population? Why do you believe this? Distinguish those parts of your rationale that are facts from those that are values. Can you pinpoint the facts versus the values in the text's argument about the future of world population?

2. In this exercise, we are going to examine in some detail a set of population projections made by the World Bank for certain countries. First, the World Bank made a set of projections for ten countries under two standard assumptions:

   a. Mortality will continue to fall everywhere in the world until life expectancy for females is 82 years. This assumption continues trends already under way in the ten largest developing countries but ignores the possibility of a major catastrophe such as war or disease.

   b. Fertility will eventually reach and stay at replacement level everywhere. For most countries for which projections were made, projected declines in fertility to replacement level extend declines that have been happening for several years. For some, such as Nigeria, where no decline had begun when the World Bank made its projections, it was assumed that fertility would start to fall in the near future.

   The World Bank then made two more sets of projections for the ten countries, under two different sets of assumptions. Under the first variation, it was assumed that fertility would fall more rapidly, while mortality would fall at the same rate as under the standard assumptions. Under the second variation, both fertility and mortality would fall more rapidly than under the standard assumptions. Both the rapid decline in fertility and the rapid decline in mortality were designed to match rapid declines that occurred in some Third World countries between 1950 and 1980.

The results of the three sets of projections for Nigeria, India, Kenya, and Mexico are shown in Table 3, with population figures for 2000 and 2050. The World Bank made these projections based on 1982 data, so the 1982 populations of the four countries are also given.

Based on the data in the table, answer the following questions.

a. How much smaller would Nigeria's population be in 2000 if fertility in that country fell rapidly (with a standard decline in mortality) rather than at the standard rate? Answer these questions for Nigeria in 2050 also. You might present these answers in tabular form.

b. Answer the same questions for India, Kenya, and Mexico.

c. Summarize in verbal form what these numbers mean—what relationships do they suggest between population growth and the magnitude and timing of declines in fertility?

d. What do these peculiarities of fertility decline and population growth suggest for government action intended to curb population growth?

Discussion

Exercise 1 was intended to provoke thought and discussion. For Exercise 2, students can work out the numbers themselves. The point of the exercise is to illustrate that the demographic impact of slow versus rapid fertility decline gets larger and larger as more time passes; in other words, delays in reducing fertility now do not have as much impact in additional population growth in the near future as they do in the more distant future. Vigorous fertility-reduction efforts introduced now earn more of their demographic payoff (reduced numbers of people over what would have occurred) in the distant future than in the near term. Thus the incentive to reduce fertility lies in the future, while the disincentive—resistance to the government—is present now. This mismatch works to discourage governments from instituting policies and programs that reduce fertility, absent other compelling circumstances.

		Population in 2000			Population in 2050		
Country	1982 Population	(A)	(B)	(C)	(A)	(B)	(C)
India	717	994	927	938	1,513	1,313	1,406
Kenya	18	40	34	35	120	69	73
Mexico	73	109	101	101	182	155	160
Nigeria	91	169	143	147	471	243	265

Table 3
Projections of Population Size (in Millions) in Selected Countries

(A) = standard fertility and mortality decline
(B) = rapid fertility decline and standard mortality decline
(C) = rapid fertility and mortality decline

VI
Population in Context

Throughout this module, the importance of population growth to global change has been assumed. Now another point is apt. While the cause of curbing global change is probably lost without population stabilization, unfortunately, population stabilization is not enough to curb global change.

Illustrating this point is a graph of the U.N. 1990 medium projection compared with its 1980 medium projection (Figure 5). The 1990 projection was discussed in the previous section; it suggests that at the "most probable" rate of fertility decline as of 1990, world population would pass 10 billion in 2050 and stabilize at just over 11.6 billion 100 years later. This projection was actually a revision of a medium projection made in 1980 by the United Nations and thought to be the most probable at that time. The 1980 projection suggested that the world's population would reach 10 billion in 2085 and stabilize eventually at 10.2 billion. The upward revision in 1990 reflects the fact that fertility declines slowed in significant areas in the decade of the 1980s, notably in China and India, falling less rapidly than the U.N. staff thought most likely in 1980.

The current world population is also shown on the graph, by the dashed line. It is perhaps not necessary to say that at this number of people, 5.4 billion, the Earth is experiencing enormous environmental damage. If the world mustered an unprecedented effort, multiplied annual expenditures on family planning, and worked hard to improve the status of women and the health of mothers and children, as discussed in previous sections, perhaps it would be possible to stabilize the world's population

at about 10 billion, instead of the 11.6 billion that the U.N. considers more likely now. If the world accomplished that unprecedented task, all that effort would mean 1.6 billion fewer people than if we only made the still very large effort required to achieve stabilization at 11.6 billion people. That number—1.6 billion people—is nearly 30% of the world's 1992 population and is indeed impressive. But without other efforts, without changing how we extract materials from the Earth's crust, how we till the soil, how we treat forests, fisheries, and water supplies, and how we spew wastes into the environment, will the environment notice that 1.6 billion-person difference? "Less than would have been" is an abstract notion indeed. To the environment, there would be nearly twice as many people as the 5.4 billion already stressing it today.

The point is that, even with enormous effort to curb population growth and achieve stabilization, it is necessary to act on the "pollution per person" and "activity per person" elements of the equations presented in the introduction to this module if the forces that currently produce global change are to be slowed or eliminated. The reason is the long time scale on which demographic change takes place; we are not likely to see negative population growth on a global scale on time scales shorter than centuries without undesirable, sharp increases in deaths.

Thus, stabilizing world population will not, by itself, avert enormous global change. Yet it is necessary. Continued population growth makes it more difficult to do all the things that a wide consensus agrees need to get done, from improving energy and materials efficiencies to raising the status of women. The following examples illustrate why.

It is widely agreed that fossil fuels play a critical role in a number of features of global change, from climate change to urban air pollution and land pollution. Thus, energy efficiency is a good idea, as well as a cost-effective one. An annual increase in energy efficiency in the United States of 1.5% is generally considered conservative and therefore reasonable. What would current U.S. population growth do to this hypothetical increase in energy efficiency? The relatively low natural increase of 0.8% would eat up more than half a gain of 1.5% in energy efficiency. Thus the United States would have to work twice as hard—year after year—to get a real effect *with* population growth as it would at zero growth.

And, as we know, natural increase ignores immigration into the United States, which current estimates suggest would bring the total growth to at least 1.0% a year. That would eat up two-thirds of a 1.5% efficiency gain. And this is in the United States, a rich and relatively slowly growing country. Compare India, where investments in energy efficiency come much harder because they must compete with other compelling social needs in a country where income per capita is a small fraction of that in the United States. India would have to exceed 2.0% energy efficiency gains every year to overcome population growth.

Another example derives from U.N. estimates. If the low projection were achieved—a peak world population of 8 billion in 2050, with declines thereafter—carbon dioxide emissions from the energy sector alone would be 3.4 billion tons less than under the medium projection (with a 2050 population of 10 billion) and 7.4 billion tons less than the high projection (with a 2050 population of 12.5 billion). The 7.4-billion-ton saving is more than the total emissions of carbon dioxide from the energy sector in 1985, and this does not take into account

improvements in efficiency and production technologies.

The effect of population growth on social efforts of the past illustrates how continued population growth requires ever greater efforts to improve conditions. The United Nations reports that the proportion of people who were malnourished in developing countries fell between 1970 and 1985, from roughly a quarter to a fifth of people. Yet the total *number* of malnourished people rose by more than 10%. Similarly, while the number of children in primary school in developing countries increased 1.5 times in the same period, the total number of children not in school in developing countries also increased.

Thus, while it is not possible to combat global change effectively by curbing population growth alone, it is also not possible to combat global change without stabilizing world population.

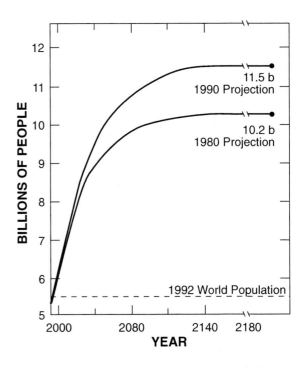

Figure 5. U.N. world population projections, made in 1980 and 1990, from 1990.

GLOSSARY

acceptor—In the context of a family planning program, an individual who agrees to use a particular birth control method or to be sterilized.

age-sex structure—A population's composition of men and women at various ages. See also **population pyramid**.

birth control—Practices used by couples to avoid conception.

carrying capacity—The number of organisms that can be supported indefinitely in a particular area or by a particular resource. Populations greater than this number are likely to degrade the environment and its resources, resulting eventually in a loss of population when impoverished resources cannot support the original number.

childbearing years—The years of a woman's life during which she is capable of conceiving and bearing children. Customarily set for statistical purposes at 15–44 (in the United States) or 15–49 (elsewhere).

child mortality rate—The number of deaths of children before age five per 1,000 infants born alive in a population.

cohort—A group of people sharing a particular demographic characteristic, such as age. The baby-boom cohort in the United States, for example, is by convention the group born between 1946 and 1966.

crude birth rate—The number of births per 1,000 people in a population.

crude death rate—The number of deaths per 1,000 people in a population.

demographic transition theory—The notion that births and deaths have undergone changes in the long sweep of history, changes that define three stages. In earliest times, both birth and death rates were high with low growth rates; later, death rates fell but fertility stayed high so that growth rates were also high; finally, birth rates fell to match death rates, producing another period of low growth but at low birth and death rates.

demography—The study of human populations.

dieback—A sharp increase in deaths in a population, causing rapid negative growth and a sharp drop in total population.

doubling time—The length of time it takes a population to double in size.

emigration—The movement of people out of a particular geographical or political area. Also "out-migration."

family planning—The conscious effort, with or without medical or mechanical intervention, to control the number and spacing of one's children, either to avoid conception or to encourage it. See also **birth control**.

fecundity—The physiological capacity of a woman or man to produce a live child.

fertility—In qualitative terms, the pattern of child bearing in a group or population. For specific quantitative measures of fertility, see **crude birth rate** and **total fertility rate**.

growth rate—See **natural increase**.

immigration—The movement of people into a particular geographical or political area. Also "in-migration."

infant mortality rate—The number of deaths before age one per 1,000 infants born alive in a population.

informed consent—In the family planning context, knowledgeable acceptance of birth control or a sterilization operation. Knowledge usually means full understanding of the medical risks involved, of the range of alternatives available, that the object is prevention of conception, and that sterilization is a permanent surgical procedure.

maternal mortality rate—The number of pregnancy-related maternal deaths per 100,000 live births in a population.

migration—The movement of people across a boundary for the purpose of establishing residence. Usually involves either international migration (between countries) or internal migration (within a country).

mortality—In qualitative terms, the pattern of death in a group or population. For specific quantitative measures of mortality, see **crude death rate**, **infant mortality rate**, **child mortality rate**, and **maternal mortality rate**.

natural increase—The excess of births over deaths in a population in a given time period. Usually cited as a rate, or as a

percentage of the total population at a particular moment, usually at midyear. Growth of a population without regard for in-migration and out-migration.

population—In the context of this module, a group of human beings.

population growth—The excess of births plus in-migrants over deaths plus out-migrants in a population in a given time period. Usually cited as a rate, or as a percentage of the total population at a particular moment, usually at midyear. Sometimes used incorrectly as a synonym for natural increase.

population policy—Governmental actions, including statements, orders, laws, regulations, treaties, and other official proclamations, as well as omissions to act that affect fertility, mortality, migration, population density, population distribution, and other aspects of population.

population projection—Calculation of future population numbers and composition, given certain assumptions about fertility, mortality, and migration levels and trends.

population pyramid—A horizontal bar chart of a population's age-sex composition.

population stabilization—In this module, a term used synonymously with zero population growth, meaning that births plus in-migrants equals deaths plus out-migrants in a given population.

replacement-level fertility—An average fertility level at which the parent generation just replaces itself, with one child for each adult. Roughly equal in the United States to a total fertility rate of 2.1.

stable population—Technically, a population with an unchanging rate of growth and unchanging age composition, the result of birth and death rates remaining constant over a sufficient length of time. Used popularly (and incorrectly) as synonymous with zero population growth.

total fertility rate—The average number of children that would be born alive to a woman (or group of women) during her lifetime if she were to pass through her childbearing years conforming to the fertility rates of a given year.

undue influence—The improper or wrongful constraint or persuasion of an individual so that the will of that individual is overridden and she or he behaves in a way contrary to how she or he would behave if left to act freely. In the family planning context, undue influence occurs when an individual's voluntary, informed consent is not given or is overridden prior to the use of birth control or the performance of a sterilization operation.

zero population growth—The state in which a population experiences no growth, or births plus in-migrants equal deaths plus out-migrants. See also **population stabilization**.

Note: Many of these are standard definitions of widely used terms. See, e.g., the glossary of Haupt and Kane, cited in the supplementary reading materials.

SUPPLEMENTARY READING

Brown, Lester. Analyzing the demographic trap. In Lester Brown, et al., eds., *State of the World 1987*. New York: W.W. Norton and Co., 1987.

————. Stopping population growth. In Lester Brown, et al., eds., *State of the World 1984*. New York: W.W. Norton and Co., 1985.

Coale, Ansley. Recent trends in fertility in less developed countries, *Science 221 (1983):* 828–832.

Ehrlich, Paul, and Anne Ehrlich. *The Population Explosion*. New York: Simon and Schuster, 1990.

Harrison, Paul. *The Third Revolution*. New York: St. Martin's Press, 1992.

Haupt, Arthur, and Thomas Kane. *The Population Reference Bureau's Population Handbook*, 3d ed. Washington, D.C.: Population Reference Bureau, 1991.

Jacobsen, Judith. *Promoting Population Stabilization: Incentives for Small Families*. Washington, D.C.: Worldwatch Institute, 1983.

Jacobson, Jodi. Planning the global family. In Lester Brown et al., eds., *State of the World 1988*. New York: W.W. Norton and Co., 1988.

McEvedy, Colin, and Richard Jones. *Atlas of World Population History*. Harmondsworth, England: Penguin Books, Ltd., 1985.

Newman, James, and Gordon Matzke. *Population: Patterns, Dynamics, and Prospects*. Englewood Cliffs, New Jersey: Prentice-Hall, 1984.

UNFPA/United Nations Population Fund. *The State of World Population 1992*. New York: UNFPA/United Nations Population Fund, 1992.

United Nations Children's Fund (UNICEF). *The State of the World's Children 1990*. Oxford: Oxford University Press, 1990.

Watkins, Susan, and Jane Menken. Famines in historical perspective. *Population and Development Review 11 (1985):* 647–675.

World Bank. Slowing population growth. In *World Development Report 1984*. New York: Oxford University Press, 1984.

1995 WORLD POPULATION DATA SHEET

	Population mid-1995 (millions)	Birth Rate per 1000 pop.	Death Rate per 1000 pop.	Natural Increase (annual, %)	"Doubling Time" in Years at Current Rate	Projected Population (millions) 2010	Projected Population (millions) 2025	Infant Mortality Rate[a]	Total Fertility Rate[b]	% Age <15	% Age 65+	Life Expectancy at Birth (years) T	M	F	% Urban	Data Code[c]	% Married Women Using Contraception Total	Modern	Govt. View of Birth Rate[d]	Per Capita GNP, 1993 (US$)
WORLD	5,702	24	9	1.5	45	7,024	8,312	62	3.1	32	6	66	64	68	43		58	49		4,500
MORE DEVELOPED	1,169	12	10	0.2	432	1,232	1,271	10	1.6	20	13	74	70	78	74		—	52		17,270
LESS DEVELOPED	4,533	28	9	1.9	36	5,791	7,041	67	3.5	35	5	64	62	65	35		55	49		1,030
LESS DEVELOPED (Excl. China)	3,314	31	9	2.2	32	4,406	5,518	72	4.0	38	4	62	60	63	37		41	33		1,250
AFRICA	720	41	13	2.8	24	1,069	1,510	90	5.8	45	3	55	53	56	31		22	17		660
SUB-SAHARAN AFRICA	586	44	14	3.0	23	892	1,290	95	6.2	46	3	52	51	54	27		15	11		560
NORTHERN AFRICA	162	32	8	2.4	29	219	279	63	4.4	41	3	64	63	65	45		39	35		1,040
Algeria	28.4	30	6	2.4	29	38.0	47.2	55	4.4	39	4	67	66	68	50	B	47	43	H	1,650
Egypt	61.9	30	8	2.3	31	80.7	97.9	62	3.9	40	4	64	62	65	44	B	47	45	H	660
Libya	5.2	42	8	3.4	21	8.9	14.4	68	6.4	48	3	63	62	65	85	B	—	—	S	—
Morocco	29.2	28	6	2.2	32	38.4	47.4	57	4.0	40	4	69	67	71	47	B	42	36	H	1,030
Sudan	28.1	41	12	3.0	23	41.5	58.4	77	5.9	46	2	55	54	56	27	B	9	6	H	—
Tunisia	8.9	25	6	1.9	36	11.2	13.3	43	3.4	37	5	68	67	69	60	B	50	40	H	1,780
Western Sahara	0.2	47	18	2.8	24	0.3	0.4	148	6.9	—	—	47	46	48	—	D	—	—	—	—
WESTERN AFRICA	199	45	14	3.1	22	311	466.8	86	6.4	46	3	53	52	55	23		8	4		370
Benin	5.4	49	18	3.1	22	8.3	12.3	86	7.1	47	3	48	46	49	30	B	9	1	S	420
Burkina Faso	10.4	47	19	2.8	24	14.5	20.9	94	6.9	48	3	45	44	46	15	B	8	4	H	300
Cape Verde	0.4	36	9	2.8	25	0.6	0.7	50	4.3	45	6	65	64	66	44	B	—	—	H	870
Côte d'Ivoire	14.3	50	15	3.5	20	23.1	36.8	92	7.4	47	2	51	50	52	39	B	3	1	S	630
Gambia	1.1	48	21	2.7	26	1.5	2.1	90	5.9	45	2	45	43	47	26	B	12	7	H	360
Ghana	17.5	42	12	3.0	23	26.6	38.0	81	5.5	45	3	56	54	58	36	B	19	9	H	430
Guinea	6.5	44	19	2.4	29	9.3	12.9	143	5.8	44	3	44	42	47	29	C	—	—	H	510
Guinea-Bissau	1.1	43	21	2.1	32	1.5	2.0	140	5.8	43	3	44	42	45	22	C	—	—	H	220
Liberia	3.0	47	14	3.3	21	4.8	7.2	126	6.8	46	4	55	54	57	44	B	6	5	H	—
Mali	9.4	51	20	3.2	22	15.0	23.7	104	7.3	46	4	47	45	48	22	B	5	1	H	300
Mauritania	2.3	40	14	2.5	27	3.3	4.4	101	5.4	45	4	52	50	53	39	B	4	1	S	510
Niger	9.2	53	19	3.4	21	14.8	22.4	123	7.4	49	3	47	45	48	15	B	4	2	H	270
Nigeria	101.2	43	12	3.1	22	162.0	246.0	72	6.3	45	3	56	55	58	16	B	6	4	H	310
Senegal	8.3	43	16	2.7	26	12.2	16.9	68	6.0	45	3	49	48	50	39	B	7	5	H	730
Sierra Leone	4.5	46	19	2.7	26	6.4	8.7	143	6.2	44	3	46	44	47	35	C	—	—	H	140
Togo	4.4	47	11	3.6	19	7.4	11.7	86	6.9	49	2	58	56	60	30	B	34	3	S	330
EASTERN AFRICA	226	46	15	3.0	23	345	491	106	6.4	47	3	50	48	52	21		17	12		210
Burundi	6.4	46	16	3.0	23	9.5	13.5	102	6.6	46	4	50	48	52	6	B	9	1	H	180
Comoros	0.5	46	11	3.6	20	0.9	1.4	79	6.8	48	3	58	56	60	29	C	—	—	H	520
Djibouti	0.6	38	16	2.2	32	0.8	1.1	115	5.8	41	2	48	47	50	77	C	—	—	S	780
Eritrea	3.5	42	16	2.6	27	5.2	7.0	135	5.8	—	—	48	46	49	17	D	—	—	H	—
Ethiopia	56.0	46	16	3.1	23	90.0	129.7	120	7.0	49	3	50	48	52	15	B	4	3	H	100
Kenya	28.3	45	12	3.3	21	43.6	63.6	69	5.7	48	3	56	54	57	27	B	33	27	H	270
Madagascar	14.8	44	12	3.2	22	23.3	34.4	93	6.1	46	3	57	55	58	22	B	17	5	H	240
Malawi	9.7	47	20	2.7	25	14.7	21.3	134	6.7	48	3	45	44	45	17	B	13	7	H	220

33

	Population mid-1995 (millions)	Birth Rate per 1000 pop.	Death Rate per 1000 pop.	Natural Increase (annual, %)	"Doubling Time" in Years at Current Rate	Projected Population (millions) 2010	Projected Population (millions) 2025	Infant Mortality Rate[a]	Total Fertility Rate[b]	% Age <15	% Age 65+	Life Expectancy at Birth (years) T	Life Expectancy at Birth (years) M	Life Expectancy at Birth (years) F	% Urban	Data Code[c]	% Married Women Using Contraception Total	% Married Women Using Contraception Modern	Govt. View of Birth Rate[d]	Per Capita GNP, 1993 (US$)
EASTERN AFRICA (continued)																				
Mauritius	1.1	21	7	1.5	47	1.3	1.5	19	2.4	30	6	69	65	73	44	A	75	49	S	2,980
Mozambique	17.4	45	19	2.7	26	26.9	38.3	148	6.5	46	2	46	45	48	33	C	—	—	H	80
Reunion	0.7	23	6	1.8	40	0.8	0.9	8	2.3	31	6	73	69	77	73	B	67	62	—	—
Rwanda	7.8	40	17	2.3	30	10.4	12.8	117	6.2	48	3	46	45	48	5	B	21	13	H	200
Seychelles	0.1	23	7	1.5	46	0.1	0.1	12	2.7	32	7	70	68	73	50	A	—	—	H	6,370
Somalia	9.3	50	19	3.2	22	14.5	21.3	122	7.0	48	3	47	45	49	24	C	—	—	S	—
Tanzania	28.5	45	15	3.0	23	42.8	58.6	92	6.3	47	3	49	47	50	21	B	20	13	H	100
Uganda	21.3	52	19	3.3	21	32.3	48.1	115	7.3	47	3	45	44	46	11	B	5	3	H	190
Zambia	9.1	47	17	3.1	23	13.0	17.1	107	6.5	50	2	48	47	49	42	B	15	9	H	370
Zimbabwe	11.3	39	12	2.7	26	15.3	19.6	53	4.4	44	3	54	52	55	27	B	48	42	H	540
MIDDLE AFRICA	83	46	16	2.9	24	127	191	107	6.3	46	3	49	47	51	33		—	—		—
Angola	11.5	47	20	2.7	26	17.6	24.7	137	6.4	45	3	46	44	48	37	D	—	—	H	—
Cameroon	13.5	40	11	2.9	24	21.2	32.6	65	5.9	44	3	58	56	60	41	B	16	4	H	770
Central African Republic	3.2	42	22	2.0	34	3.9	5.2	136	5.3	43	4	41	40	43	39	C	—	—	H	390
Chad	6.4	44	18	2.6	27	9.3	12.9	122	5.9	41	3	48	46	49	22	C	—	—	S	200
Congo	2.5	40	17	2.3	31	3.2	4.2	109	5.2	44	3	46	44	48	58	C	—	—	H	920
Equatorial Guinea	0.4	40	14	2.6	27	0.6	0.9	99	5.3	43	4	53	51	56	37	C	—	—	S	360
Gabon	1.3	37	16	2.2	32	1.9	2.7	94	4.0	39	6	54	52	55	73	C	—	—	L	4,050
Sao Tome and Principe	0.1	35	9	2.6	27	0.2	0.2	62	4.4	47	4	64	62	66	46	A	—	—	H	330
Zaire	44.1	48	16	3.2	22	69.1	107.6	108	6.6	48	3	48	46	50	29	B	8	3	S	—
SOUTHERN AFRICA	50	31	8	2.3	30	67	83	49	4.2	38	4	65	62	67	59		50	48		2,720
Botswana	1.5	31	7	2.3	30	2.2	3.0	39	4.2	43	3	64	60	66	27	B	33	32	H	2,590
Lesotho	2.1	31	12	1.9	36	3.0	4.2	79	5.2	41	4	61	58	63	22	B	23	19	H	660
Namibia	1.5	37	10	2.7	26	2.2	3.0	57	5.4	42	4	59	58	60	32	B	29	26	H	1,660
South Africa	43.5	31	8	2.3	30	57.5	70.1	46	4.1	37	5	66	63	68	63	B	53	52	H	2,900
Swaziland	1.0	43	11	3.2	22	1.6	2.5	90	6.1	46	2	57	53	61	30	B	20	17	H	1,050
ASIA	3,451	24	8	1.7	42	4,242	4,939	62	2.9	33	5	65	64	67	33		62	55		1,980
ASIA (Excl. China)	2,232	28	9	1.9	36	2,857	3,416	68	3.5	36	5	63	62	64	35		45	35		2,860
WESTERN ASIA	168	31	7	2.4	29	242	329	51	4.3	39	4	67	65	69	58		—	—		—
Armenia	3.7	16	7	0.8	83	4.2	4.3	17	2.0	31	7	71	68	74	68	B	—	12	S	660
Azerbaijan	7.3	23	7	1.6	43	9.0	10.3	26	2.5	33	5	71	66	75	54	B	—	7	S	730
Bahrain	0.6	29	4	2.5	28	0.8	1.1	25	3.7	32	2	74	71	76	88	B	54	30	S	7,870
Cyprus	0.7	17	8	0.9	76	0.8	0.9	9	2.3	25	11	77	75	79	68	C	—	—	L	10,380
Gaza	0.9	52	6	4.6	15	1.8	2.8	34	8.1	50	4	69	68	69	94	C	—	—	—	—
Georgia	5.4	12	10	0.2	462	5.7	6.0	18	1.5	25	10	73	69	76	56	B	—	8	S	560
Iraq	20.6	43	7	3.7	19	34.5	52.6	62	6.6	47	3	66	65	67	70	C	18	10	L	—
Israel	5.5	21	6	1.5	47	6.9	8.0	7	2.8	30	9	77	75	79	90	A	—	—	L	13,760
Jordan	4.1	38	4	3.3	21	6.2	8.3	32	5.6	43	3	72	70	74	68	B	35	27	H	1,190
Kuwait	1.5	25	2	2.2	31	2.5	3.6	12	4.0	34	2	75	73	77	—	C	35	32	S	23,350
Lebanon	3.7	25	5	2.0	34	5.0	6.1	28	2.9	33	5	75	73	78	86	D	65	39	S	—
Oman	2.2	53	4	4.9	14	3.7	6.0	24	6.9	36	3	71	70	72	12	C	9	8	S	5,600
Qatar	0.5	19	2	1.8	39	0.6	0.7	13	3.8	30	1	73	70	75	91	B	26	24	S	15,140
Saudi Arabia	18.5	36	4	3.2	22	30.0	48.2	24	5.5	43	2	70	69	72	79	C	—	—	S	7,780
Syria	14.7	41	6	3.5	20	23.6	33.5	39	5.9	49	4	66	65	67	51	C	—	—	S	—
Turkey	61.4	23	7	1.6	44	79.2	95.6	53	2.7	33	4	67	64	70	51	B	63	35	H	2,120
United Arab Emirates	1.9	23	4	1.9	36	2.5	3.0	23	4.1	32	1	72	70	74	82	C	—	—	S	22,470
West Bank	1.5	41	7	3.4	20	2.7	3.8	38	5.7	46	4	68	68	68	—	C	—	—	—	—
Yemen	13.2	50	14	3.6	19	21.9	34.5	109	7.7	52	3	52	52	53	25	B	10	6	H	—

	Population mid-1995 (millions)	Birth Rate per 1000 pop.	Death Rate per 1000 pop.	Natural Increase (annual, %)	"Doubling Time" in Years at Current Rate	Projected Population (millions) 2010	Projected Population (millions) 2025	Infant Mortality Rate[a]	Total Fertility Rate[b]	% Age <15	% Age 65+	Life Expectancy at Birth (years) T	M	F	% Urban	Data Code[c]	% Married Women Using Contraception Total	Modern	Govt. View of Birth Rate[d]	Per Capita GNP, 1993 (US$)
SOUTH CENTRAL ASIA	1,355	31	10	2.1	33	1,772	2,138	79	3.8	38	4	60	60	61	27		39	30		420
Afghanistan	18.4	50	22	2.8	24	31.1	41.4	163	6.9	41	3	43	43	44	18	D	—	—	H	—
Bangladesh	119.2	36	12	2.4	29	160.8	194.1	108	4.3	42	3	55	56	55	17	B	45	36	H	220
Bhutan	0.8	39	15	2.3	30	1.1	1.5	138	6.2	39	4	51	51	50	13	D	—	—	S	170
India	930.6	29	9	1.9	36	1,182.7	1,384.6	74	3.4	36	4	60	60	60	26	B	41	37	H	290
Iran	61.3	36	7	2.9	24	83.7	106.1	56	5.0	44	3	67	66	68	57	B	65	45	H	2,230
Kazakhstan	16.9	19	9	0.9	74	18.4	20.5	28	2.3	31	6	69	64	73	57	B	—	22	S	1,540
Kyrgyzstan	4.4	26	8	1.8	38	5.6	7.0	33	3.3	38	5	68	64	72	36	B	—	25	S	830
Maldives	0.3	43	7	3.6	19	0.4	0.6	52	6.2	47	3	65	64	67	26	B	—	—	S	820
Nepal	22.6	38	14	2.4	29	32.2	43.3	102	5.8	42	3	54	56	53	10	B	23	22	H	160
Pakistan	129.7	39	10	2.9	24	187.7	251.8	91	5.6	41	3	61	61	61	32	C	12	9	H	430
Sri Lanka	18.2	21	6	1.5	46	21.0	24.0	19	2.3	35	4	73	70	75	22	A	66	44	H	600
Tajikistan	5.8	33	9	2.4	29	9.2	13.1	47	4.3	43	4	70	68	73	31	B	—	15	H	470
Turkmenistan	4.5	33	8	2.5	28	5.9	7.9	44	4.0	41	4	66	63	70	45	B	—	12	S	1,380
Uzbekistan	22.7	31	7	2.5	28	31.9	42.3	37	3.8	41	4	69	66	72	41	B	—	19	S	960
SOUTHEAST ASIA	485	26	8	1.9	37	601	704	53	3.2	37	4	64	62	66	31		51	44		1,070
Brunei	0.3	27	3	2.4	29	0.4	0.4	7	3.1	36	3	74	73	76	67	A	—	—	S	—
Cambodia	10.6	44	16	2.8	25	15.7	22.8	108	5.8	46	3	50	48	51	13	D	—	—	H	—
Indonesia	198.4	24	8	1.6	43	240.6	276.5	64	2.8	37	4	63	61	65	31	B	50	47	H	730
Laos	4.8	42	14	2.8	25	7.2	9.8	98	6.0	45	3	52	51	54	19	B	—	—	S	290
Malaysia	19.9	29	5	2.4	29	27.5	34.5	12	3.3	36	4	71	69	74	51	B	56	37	H	3,160
Myanmar	44.8	28	9	1.9	36	57.3	69.3	48	3.6	36	4	60	58	63	25	C	—	—	H	—
Philippines	68.4	30	9	2.1	33	87.2	102.7	49	4.1	40	3	65	63	66	49	B	40	25	H	830
Singapore	3.0	17	5	1.2	56	3.6	4.0	5	1.8	23	7	74	72	77	100	A	65	—	L	19,310
Thailand	60.2	20	6	1.4	48	68.7	75.4	35	2.2	31	4	70	68	72	19	B	66	64	H	2,040
Viet Nam	75.0	30	7	2.3	30	92.5	108.1	42	3.7	39	5	65	63	67	21	B	49	37	H	170
EAST ASIA	1,442	17	6	1.0	66	1,628	1,768	40	1.8	26	7	70	68	72	35		87	84		3,570
China	1,218.8	18	6	1.1	62	1,385.5	1,522.8	44	1.9	27	6	69	67	70	28	B	90	89	S	490
Hong Kong	6.0	12	5	0.7	99	6.4	6.3	5	1.2	20	9	78	75	81	—	A	81	75	—	17,860
Japan	125.2	10	7	0.3	277	130.4	125.8	4	1.5	16	14	79	76	83	77	A	64	47	L	31,450
Korea, North	23.5	23	6	1.8	40	28.5	32.1	26	2.4	30	4	70	67	73	61	D	—	—	S	—
Korea, South	44.9	15	6	1.0	72	49.7	50.8	11	1.6	24	5	72	68	76	74	B	79	69	S	7,670
Macao	0.4	16	4	1.2	57	0.5	0.6	9	1.6	24	7	—	—	—	97	B	—	—	—	—
Mongolia	2.3	22	8	1.4	51	3.0	3.6	61	3.8	40	4	64	62	65	55	C	—	—	S	400
Taiwan	21.2	16	5	1.0	67	24.0	25.5	6	1.8	25	7	74	72	77	75	A	75	68	—	—
NORTH AMERICA	293	15	9	0.7	105	334	375	8	2.0	22	13	76	72	79	75		71	66		24,340
Canada	29.6	14	7	0.7	102	33.6	36.6	7	1.7	21	12	78	74	81	77	A	73	69	S	20,670
United States	263.2	15	9	0.7	105	300.4	338.3	8	2.0	22	13	76	72	79	75	A	71	65	S	24,750
LATIN AMERICA AND THE CARIBBEAN	481	26	7	1.9	36	601	706	44	3.1	34	5	69	66	72	70		61	51		3,040
CENTRAL AMERICA	126	29	5	2.3	30	163	196	37	3.5	37	4	71	68	74	65		60	51		3,090
Belize	0.2	38	5	3.3	21	0.3	0.4	34	4.5	44	4	68	67	71	48	B	47	42	H	2,440
Costa Rica	3.3	26	4	2.2	32	4.4	5.5	14	3.1	35	5	76	74	79	49	A	75	65	H	2,160
El Salvador	5.9	32	6	2.6	27	7.6	9.4	41	3.8	40	4	68	65	70	46	B	53	48	H	1,320
Guatemala	10.6	39	8	3.1	22	15.8	21.7	48	5.4	45	3	65	62	67	38	C	23	19	H	1,110
Honduras	5.5	34	6	2.8	25	7.6	9.7	50	5.2	47	4	68	66	71	46	B	47	34	H	580
Mexico	93.7	27	5	2.2	34	117.7	136.6	34	3.1	36	4	72	70	76	71	B	65	56	H	3,750
Nicaragua	4.4	33	6	2.7	26	6.7	9.1	49	4.6	46	3	65	62	68	62	C	49	45	H	360
Panama	2.6	29	8	2.1	33	3.3	3.8	28	3.0	34	5	72	69	75	54	B	58	54	S	2,580

	Population mid-1995 (millions)	Birth Rate per 1000 pop.	Death Rate per 1000 pop.	Natural Increase (annual, %)	"Doubling Time" in Years at Current Rate	Projected Population (millions) 2010	Projected Population (millions) 2025	Infant Mortality Rate[a]	Total Fertility Rate[b]	% Age <15	% Age 65+	Life Expectancy at Birth (years) T	Life Expectancy M	Life Expectancy F	% Urban	Data Code[c]	% Married Women Using Contraception Total	% Married Women Using Contraception Modern	Govt. View of Birth Rate[d]	Per Capita GNP, 1993 (US$)
CARIBBEAN	36	23	8	1.5	46	43	50	39	2.9	31	7	70	67	72	60		—	—		—
Antigua and Barbuda	0.1	18	6	1.2	58	0.1	0.1	18	1.7	25	6	73	71	75	31	A	53	51	S	6,390
Bahamas	0.3	20	5	1.5	47	0.3	0.4	24	2.0	29	5	73	69	78	84	A	62	60	S	11,500
Barbados	0.3	16	9	0.7	98	0.3	0.3	9	1.8	24	12	76	73	78	38	A	55	53	S	6,240
Cuba	11.2	14	7	0.7	102	12.3	12.9	9	1.8	22	9	75	72	78	74	A	—	—	S	—
Dominica	0.1	20	7	1.3	55	0.1	0.1	18	2.5	29	8	77	74	80	—	A	50	48	H	2,680
Dominican Republic	7.8	27	6	2.1	32	9.7	11.2	42	3.3	35	4	70	68	72	61	B	56	52	H	1,080
Grenada	0.1	29	6	2.4	29	0.1	0.2	12	3.8	43	5	71	68	73	—	B	54	49	H	2,410
Guadeloupe	0.4	18	6	1.2	56	0.5	0.5	10	2.0	26	8	75	71	78	48	A	—	—	—	—
Haiti	7.2	35	12	2.3	30	9.8	13.1	74	4.8	40	4	57	55	58	31	B	18	14	H	—
Jamaica	2.4	25	6	2.0	35	2.8	3.3	13	2.4	33	8	74	71	76	53	A	67	63	H	1,390
Martinique	0.4	17	6	1.1	62	0.4	0.5	8	2.0	23	10	76	73	79	81	B	—	—	—	—
Netherlands Antilles	0.2	19	6	1.3	55	0.2	0.2	6	2.0	26	7	76	74	79	92	A	—	—	—	—
Puerto Rico	3.7	18	8	1.0	67	4.1	4.6	13	2.2	27	10	74	70	79	73	A	70	62	—	7,020
St. Kitts-Nevis	0.04	23	9	1.4	50	0.1	0.1	19	2.5	32	9	69	66	71	42	A	41	37	H	4,470
Saint Lucia	0.1	27	6	2.0	34	0.2	0.2	19	3.1	37	7	72	68	75	48	A	47	46	H	3,040
St. Vincent and the Grenadines	0.1	25	7	1.8	38	0.1	0.2	16	3.1	37	6	73	71	74	25	A	58	55	H	2,130
Trinidad and Tobago	1.3	17	7	1.1	64	1.6	1.8	11	2.7	31	6	71	68	73	65	A	53	44	H	3,730
SOUTH AMERICA	319	25	7	1.8	38	395	460	47	3.0	33	5	68	65	71	73		64	51		3,020
Argentina	34.6	21	8	1.3	55	40.8	46.1	24	2.8	30	9	71	68	75	87	A	—	—	S	7,290
Bolivia	7.4	36	10	2.6	27	10.2	13.1	71	4.8	41	4	60	59	62	58	B	45	18	S	770
Brazil	157.8	25	8	1.7	41	194.4	224.6	58	2.9	32	5	66	64	69	77	B	66	56	S	3,020
Chile	14.3	22	6	1.7	41	17.3	20.1	15	2.5	31	6	72	69	76	85	A	—	—	S	3,070
Colombia	37.7	24	6	1.8	39	46.1	53.0	37	2.7	33	5	69	66	72	50	B	66	55	S	1,400
Ecuador	11.5	28	6	2.2	31	14.9	17.8	50	3.5	38	4	69	66	71	58	B	57	46	H	1,170
Guyana	0.8	25	7	1.8	39	1.0	1.1	48	2.6	32	4	65	62	68	33	B	—	—	S	350
Paraguay	5.0	33	6	2.8	25	7.0	9.0	38	4.3	40	4	70	68	72	51	B	48	35	S	1,500
Peru	24.0	29	7	2.1	33	30.3	35.9	60	3.5	36	4	66	64	68	70	B	59	33	H	1,490
Suriname	0.4	25	6	2.0	36	0.5	0.6	28	2.7	35	5	70	68	73	49	B	—	—	S	1,210
Uruguay	3.2	17	10	0.7	102	3.5	3.7	19	2.3	26	12	73	69	76	90	A	—	—	L	3,910
Venezuela	21.8	30	5	2.6	27	28.7	34.8	20	3.6	38	4	72	69	75	84	A	—	—	S	2,840
EUROPE	729	11	12	-0.1	—	743	743	11	1.5	20	13	73	68	77	72		—	45		11,870
NORTHERN EUROPE	94	13	11	0.2	443	97	99	7	1.8	20	15	76	73	79	85		73	66		18,020
Denmark	5.2	13	12	0.1	770	5.3	5.3	6	1.8	17	15	75	73	78	85	A	78	71	S	26,510
Estonia	1.5	9	14	-0.5	—	1.4	1.4	16	1.3	21	13	70	64	75	71	B	—	26	L	3,040
Finland	5.1	13	10	0.3	227	5.2	5.2	4	1.8	19	14	76	72	79	64	A	—	—	S	18,970
Iceland	0.3	17	7	1.1	64	0.3	0.3	5	2.2	25	11	79	77	81	91	A	—	—	S	23,620
Ireland	3.6	14	9	0.5	139	3.5	3.5	6	2.0	26	11	75	73	78	57	A	—	—	S	12,580
Latvia	2.5	10	15	-0.5	—	2.4	2.4	16	1.5	21	13	68	62	74	69	B	—	19	L	2,030
Lithuania	3.7	13	12	0.0	6931	3.8	3.9	16	1.7	22	12	71	65	76	68	B	—	12	S	1,310
Norway	4.3	14	11	0.3	224	4.7	5.0	6	1.9	19	16	77	74	80	73	A	76	65	S	26,340
Sweden	8.9	13	12	0.1	990	9.2	9.6	5	1.9	19	18	78	76	81	83	A	78	71	S	24,830
United Kingdom	58.6	13	11	0.2	385	61.0	62.1	7	1.8	19	16	76	74	79	92	A	72	71	S	17,970
WESTERN EUROPE	181	11	10	0.1	741	187	184	6	1.5	18	15	77	73	80	81		77	69		23,310
Austria	8.1	12	10	0.1	533	8.3	8.3	6	1.4	18	15	77	73	80	54	A	71	56	S	23,120
Belgium	10.2	12	11	0.1	578	10.4	10.5	8	1.6	18	16	77	73	80	97	A	79	75	S	21,210
France	58.1	12	9	0.3	217	61.7	63.6	6	1.7	20	15	78	74	82	74	A	81	66	L	22,360
Germany	81.7	10	11	-0.1	—	81.2	76.1	6	1.3	16	15	76	73	79	85	A	75	72	L	23,560
Liechtenstein	0.03	12	6	0.6	108	0.03	0.04	10.7	1.4	19	10	—	—	—	—	A	—	—	S	—
Luxembourg	0.4	13	10	0.4	193	0.4	0.4	6	1.7	18	14	76	73	79	86	A	—	—	L	35,850
Netherlands	15.5	13	9	0.4	182	16.9	17.6	6	1.6	18	13	77	74	80	89	A	76	72	S	20,710
Switzerland	7.0	12	9	0.3	224	7.6	7.5	6	1.5	16	15	78	75	81	68	A	71	65	L	36,410

	Population mid-1995 (millions)	Birth Rate per 1000 pop.	Death Rate per 1000 pop.	Natural Increase (annual, %)	"Doubling Time" in Years at Current Rate	Projected Population (millions) 2010	Projected Population (millions) 2025	Infant Mortality Rate[a]	Total Fertility Rate[b]	% Age <15	% Age 65+	Life Expectancy at Birth (years) T	Life Expectancy at Birth (years) M	Life Expectancy at Birth (years) F	% Urban	Data Code[c]	% Married Women Using Contraception Total	% Married Women Using Contraception Modern	Govt. View of Birth Rate[d]	Per Capita GNP, 1993 (US$)
EASTERN EUROPE	**310**	**10**	**14**	**–0.3**	**—**	**315**	**320**	**17**	**1.5**	**22**	**12**	**68**	**62**	**73**	**68**		**—**	**22**		**2,180**
Belarus	10.3	11	13	–0.2	—	10.9	11.3	13	1.5	22	12	69	64	74	68	B	—	13	S	2,840
Bulgaria	8.5	10	13	–0.3	—	7.9	7.5	16	1.4	19	14	71	68	74	67	A	—	—	L	1,160
Czech Republic	10.4	12	11	0.0	2310	10.5	10.7	9	1.7	21	10	73	69	77	75	A	69	45	S	2,730
Hungary	10.2	12	14	–0.3	—	9.9	9.3	12	1.7	19	14	69	65	74	63	A	73	62	L	3,330
Moldova	4.3	15	12	0.4	193	4.8	5.1	22	2.1	28	9	68	64	72	47	B	—	15	S	1,180
Poland	38.6	12	10	0.2	301	40.2	41.7	14	1.8	24	11	72	67	76	62	A	—	—	S	2,270
Romania	22.7	11	12	–0.1	—	22.2	21.6	23	1.4	22	11	70	66	73	55	A	57	15	L	1,120
Russia	147.5	9	16	–0.6	—	149.5	153.1	19	1.4	22	11	65	59	72	73	B	—	22	L	2,350
Slovakia	5.4	14	10	0.4	178	5.7	6.0	16	1.9	25	11	71	67	75	57	A	74	42	S	1,900
Ukraine	52.0	11	14	–0.4	—	53.0	54.0	15	1.6	21	13	69	64	74	68	B	—	15	L	1,910
SOUTHERN EUROPE	**144**	**11**	**9**	**0.1**	**516**	**144**	**139**	**11**	**1.4**	**18**	**14**	**76**	**73**	**79**	**60**		**—**	**—**		**14,720**
Albania	3.5	23	5	1.8	39	4.1	4.7	33	2.9	33	5	72	69	75	37	A	—	—	S	340
Bosnia-Herzegovina	3.5	14	7	0.7	95	4.4	4.5	15	1.6	23	7	72	70	75	34	—	—	—	S	—
Croatia	4.5	10	11	–0.1	—	4.4	4.2	12	1.4	19	13	70	66	75	54	A	—	—	L	—
Greece	10.5	10	9	0.0	1733	10.2	10.0	8	1.4	19	14	77	75	80	63	A	—	—	L	7,390
Italy	57.7	9	10	0.0	—	56.5	52.8	7	1.2	16	16	77	74	80	68	A	—	—	S	19,620
Macedonia	2.1	16	8	0.8	85	2.3	2.5	24	2.2	26	7	72	70	74	58	A	—	—	H	780
Malta	0.4	14	7	0.7	102	0.4	0.4	9	2.0	23	11	75	73	78	85	A	—	—	S	—
Portugal	9.9	12	11	0.1	866	9.9	9.8	9	1.5	18	14	75	71	78	34	A	—	—	L	7,890
San Marino	0.03	10	6	0.4	169	0.03	0.03	9	1.1	15	14	76	73	79	90	A	—	—	S	—
Slovenia	2.0	10	10	0.1	1386	2.0	1.9	7	1.3	19	12	73	69	77	50	A	—	—	L	6,310
Spain	39.1	10	9	0.1	578	39.0	37.1	8	1.2	17	15	77	73	81	64	A	59	38	S	13,650
Yugoslavia	10.8	13	10	0.3	204	11.1	11.5	18	2.0	23	10	72	69	75	47	A	—	—	S	—
OCEANIA	**28**	**19**	**8**	**1.2**	**60**	**34**	**39**	**24**	**2.5**	**26**	**10**	**73**	**71**	**76**	**71**		**65**	**—**		**13,540**
Australia	18.0	15	7	0.8	91	20.8	23.1	6	1.9	22	12	78	75	81	85	A	76	72	S	17,510
Federated States of Micronesia	0.1	38	8	3.0	23	0.1	0.1	52	5.6	46	4	68	66	70	26	C	—	—	H	—
Fiji	0.8	25	5	2.0	35	0.9	1.1	19	3.0	38	3	63	61	65	39	B	—	—	H	2,140
French Polynesia	0.2	26	5	2.1	34	0.3	0.4	12	3.1	36	3	70	68	72	57	B	—	—	—	—
Guam	0.2	30	4	2.6	27	0.2	0.2	10	3.3	30	4	74	72	76	38	A	—	—	—	—
Marshall Islands	0.1	49	9	4.0	17	0.1	0.2	63	7.2	51	3	63	62	65	65	B	—	—	H	—
New Caledonia	0.2	26	6	2.0	34	0.2	0.3	21	3.3	33	5	74	71	77	70	B	—	—	—	—
New Zealand	3.5	16	8	0.9	81	4.1	4.5	7	2.0	23	12	76	73	79	85	A	—	—	S	12,900
Palau	0.02	22	8	1.4	50	0.03	0.03	25	3.1	30	6	67	—	—	60	C	—	—	—	—
Papua—New Guinea	4.1	33	10	2.3	30	5.7	7.3	63	4.7	40	4	57	56	58	15	B	18	—	H	1,120
Solomon Islands	0.4	44	7	3.7	19	0.6	0.8	43	5.8	47	3	61	—	—	13	B	—	—	H	750
Vanuatu	0.2	38	9	2.9	24	0.2	0.3	45	5.3	46	3	63	—	—	18	B	—	—	S	1,230
Western Samoa	0.2	34	8	2.6	27	0.2	0.3	21	4.2	41	4	65	—	—	21	B	—	—	H	980

(—) indicates data unavailable or inapplicable

[a]Infant deaths per 1,000 live births

[b]Average number of children born to a woman in her lifetime

[c]A=complete data . . . D=little or no data

[d]H=too high, S=satisfactory, L=too low

[e]On April 27, 1992, Serbia and Montenegro formed a new state, the Federal Republic of Yugoslavia

Source: Population Reference Bureau, Inc., May 1995

Population Reference Bureau

1875 Connecticut Ave., NW, Suite 520

Washington, DC 20009 USA

Notes

The *World Population Data Sheet* lists all geo-political entities with populations of 150,000 or more and all members of the UN. These include sovereign states, dependencies, overseas departments, and some territories whose status or boundaries may be undetermined or in dispute. **More developed regions,** following the UN classification, comprise all of Europe and North America, plus Australia, Japan, and New Zealand. All other regions and countries are classified as **less developed.** This year one country, Palau, was added to the *Data Sheet* because it attained a population size of 150,000.

World and Regional Totals: Regional population totals are independently rounded and include small countries or areas not shown. Regional and world rates and percentages are weighted averages of countries for which data are available; regional averages are shown when data or estimates are available for at least three-quarters of the region's population.

World Population Data Sheets from different years should **not be used as a time series.** Fluctuations in values from year to year often reflect revisions based on new data or estimates rather than actual changes in levels. Additional information on likely trends and consistent time series can be obtained from PRB, and are available in UN, World Bank, and U.S. Census Bureau publications.

Sources

The rates and figures are primarily compiled from the following sources: official statistical yearbooks and bulletins from the countries, United Nations *Demographic Yearbook, 1993* (forthcoming) and *Population and Vital Statistics Report, Data Available as of 1 April 1995* (forthcoming) of the UN Statistical Division; *World Population Prospects: The 1994 Revision* of the UN Population Division; the UN Statistical Library; Demographic and Health Surveys; the data files and library resources of the International

Programs Center, U.S. Bureau of the Census; data from the publications of the Council of Europe and the European Communities; and long-term population projections of the World Bank. Other sources include recent demographic surveys, and special studies and direct fax and telephone communication with demographers and statistical bureaus in the United States and abroad. Specific data sources may be obtained by contacting the authors of the *Data Sheet.*

For countries with complete registration of births and deaths, rates are those most recently reported. For developed countries, nearly all vital rates refer to 1993 or 1994, and for less developed countries, for some point in the early 1990s. Completeness of vital statistics registration is indicated by the data code column on the *Data Sheet.*

Definitions

Mid-1995 Population: Estimates are based on a
  recent census, official national data, or UN,
  U.S. Census Bureau, or World Bank projections. The effects of refugee movements,
  large numbers of foreign workers, and population shifts due to contemporary political
  events are taken into account to the extent
  possible. Such events can introduce a high
  degree of uncertainty into the estimates.

Birth and Death Rate: The annual number of
  births and deaths per 1,000 total population.
  These rates are often referred to as "crude
  rates" since they do not take into account a
  population's age structure. Thus, crude
  death rates in more developed countries,
  with a relatively large proportion of older
  population, are often higher than those in
  less developed countries.

Rate of Natural Increase (RNI): Birth rate minus the death rate, implying the annual rate
  of population growth without regard for
  migration. Expressed as a percentage.

Population "Doubling Time": The number of years it will take for the population to double assuming a *constant* rate of natural increase. Based upon the *unrounded* RNI, this column provides an indication of potential growth associated with a given RNI. It is not intended to forecast the actual doubling of any population. Projections for 2010 and 2025 should be consulted for a more plausible expectation of future growth.

Population in 2010 and 2025: Projected populations based upon reasonable assumptions on the future course of fertility, mortality, and migration. Projections are based upon official country projections, or upon series issued by the UN, the U.S. Census Bureau, World Bank, or PRB projections.

Infant Mortality Rate: The annual number of deaths of infants under age one year per 1,000 live births. Rates shown with decimals are completely registered national statistics while those without are estimates from the sources cited above. Rates shown in italics are based upon less than 50 annual infant deaths and, as a result, are subject to considerable yearly variability. Rates for the republics of the former USSR omit several categories of infant deaths and may understate mortality by 20–50 percent.

Total Fertility Rate (TFR): The average number of children a woman will have assuming that current age-specific birth rates will remain constant throughout her childbearing years (usually considered to be ages 15–49).

Population Under Age 15/Age 65 or over: The percentage of the total population in those age groups, which are often considered the "dependent ages."

Life Expectancy at Birth: The average number of years a newborn infant can expect to live under *current* mortality levels.

Urban Population: Percentage of the total population living in areas termed "urban" by that country. Typically, the population living in towns of 2,000 or more or in national and provincial capitals are classified "urban."

Data Code: Provides a general indication of data availability. An "A" indicates a country with both complete vital statistics (birth and death data) and a published national level census within 10 years or a continuous population register. Countries rated "B" have one of those two sources plus either a census within 15 years or a usable national survey or sample registration system within 10 years, or both. "C" indicates that at least a census, a survey, or sample registration system is available. "D" indicates that little or no reliable demographic information is available and that estimates are based on fragmentary data or demographic models. There can be considerable variation in the quality of data even within the same category.

Contraceptive Use: The percentage of currently married or "in-union" women of reproductive age who use any form of contraception. "Modern" methods include clinic and supply methods such as the pill, IUD, condom, and sterilization. Data are the most recent available national-level surveys such as the Demographic and Health Survey programs, and United Nations Population Division, *World Contraceptive Use 1994.*

Government View of Current Birth Rate: This population policy indicator presents the officially stated position of country governments on the level of the national birth rate. Most indicators are from the United Nations Population Division, *Global Population Policy Data Base, 1993* (forthcoming).

Per Capita GNP: Gross national product includes the value of all domestic and foreign output. Estimates are from *The World Bank Atlas, 1995.* Figures in italics refer to 1992. Data on Ethiopia include Eritrea.

INDEX